DISCARD

My Grandfather's Cape Breton

CLIVE DOUCET

McGRAW-HILL RYERSON LIMITED
Toronto Halifax Montreal Vancouver

My Grandfather's Cape Breton
Copyright © Clive Doucet, 1980

ISBN 0-07-0877870-1
1 2 3 4 5 6 7 8 9 10 D 9 8 7 6 5 4 3 2 1 0

Printed and bound in Canada

Canadian Cataloguing in Publication Data

Doucet, Clive, date
My grandfather's Cape Breton

ISBN 0-07-077870-1

1. Doucet, Clive, date—Biography. 2. Authors, Canadian (English)—20th century—Biography.* I. Title.

PS8557.082Z53 1980   C813'.54   C80-094080-6
PR9199.3.D69Z46

*To my grandfather and my father,
two men whose peaceful sense of
purpose has been a constant
inspiration to me.*

Dear Grandpa:

We never really did say goodbye in any kind of final way. It was always a temporary thing until we should next meet. You were my grandfather and I was your grandson. That was the way the universe was ordered. Nothing would ever change that. It was just as sure as the sun coming up behind the mountains each morning. But many years have passed since I was that young boy who followed you around from sunrise to sunset, badgering you with a thousand questions, and you patiently shepherding your city grandson through country summer days.

It doesn't seem possible that so many years could have passed, yet they have. Time is a curious phenomenon. In one way, those days seems like an age long past and, in another way, like they were just yesterday. Through it all, I have found that the confidence and optimism I gained during those summers on the farm have remained to guide me through the difficult business of growing up. I'm not quite sure how it happened. I just know that it did and I want to say thank you.

The second reason I wanted to write this was because I've come to think that your small farm was more important than you ever gave it, or yourself credit. You were more independent than I am now, Grandpa, yet I have eighteen years of schooling behind me while you had none. It seems curious to me now that you were apologetic about your lack of "schooling." You possessed far more knowledge than most of the so-called educated people you admired, more brains and integrity than ninety-five per cent of the politicians you ever knew or heard about. "Marginal farming operations" is the name the government gave to parts of Canada like North Inverness, Cape Breton, marginal operations which had to be phased out and reforested as quickly as possible. And the fact that these people had "schooling" helped you to accept the notion that the small farm had become something of a curiosity, if not an outright albatross around the country's neck.

As a young boy I had the invaluable opportunity of seeing and feeling a small part of what Canada was like before we lost a countryside and gained an agro-industry. I no longer think the government was right, Grandpa. I no longer think bigger is better. It's difficult for me to explain to my friends the extent of what we've lost. So many of the talents and situations that you took for granted have disappeared. There are no great ruins to remind us of what has gone before, no public buildings to reconstruct. Although there were many songs sung and stories told, Grand Etang wasn't a place of writing and recording. It was a place of doing, a sensuous, physical, intimate, vibrant place that reached out and caressed your heart. You don't have the same feeling in the city. It comes from open spaces, from stability rooted in changing seasons, the growing and harvesting of crops, from people knowing each other well, from good times and bad times, from a certain pride, a sense of place, a comfortable country kitchen.

Grand Etang was a place you lived, not reflected behind a desk about living. How do you describe such communities after the people are gone? A line of houses, some grown-over pastures—it's like trying to explain what the dew is without the grass. Yet villages like Grand Etang are an integral part of where we've come from and what we are now.

Another reason I wrote the book, Grandpa, was that I was frightened, frightened that I would forget you. Strange thing to say, isn't it? Do you know that towards the end, when you were the oldest person in the village, I was terrified that you would forget me, that one day I would come stamping and helloing into the kitchen and you would say, "Who is that? Who is making all that noise?" Surely one day this would happen. You had become so fragile and I had changed a lot. But you never did forget. You always remembered me. You teased me and called me a savage because I had grown a beard and my hair was long. But the long hair and beard were just part of the camouflage of the time, the sixties. All that remains of the beard now is a moustache, and my hair, to be generous, is short.

It's been many years since I was that little boy. Who would have thought that one day I would be grown up with a wife, a house and children of my own? Yet here I am and the time has passed. It was in one of those moods when Clive at twelve began to seem like a different person that I began to be frightened that I might forget. Forget how it felt to walk out of my grandfather's house on that first warm summer morning. Forget the wonder of my first meeting with the sea sky. Forget your silver tears. Forget the happiness and sense of confidence that gradually grew inside me as I toured around after you doing what I could, watching what I couldn't do, and learning all the while to have faith in myself and my heritage.

I thought that if I could get some of it down on paper while I still remembered—get the feel of being a young boy and discovering my very own Grandpa written down—even if I did begin to forget, I could go back to the words and be reminded. Perhaps it is an impossible task that can't be fully achieved, but I'm glad I've tried.

Oh, and before I go Grandpa, I must tell you that I've finally found my dinosaur—it's me.

Much love, your grandson,

It was the summer of 1958 and I was twelve years old. . . .

Hanging On

The small turbo-prop lurched and swayed over the mountains that guarded the approach to the airport at Sydney. I had been sick once and felt like I was going to be sick again. I just wanted to go home, back to Ottawa. Other boys got sent to camp for the summer. Why was I going to see my Grandfather? I could hardly remember him and he probably wouldn't remember me. I'd just get in his way.

The plane sank into another air pocket and my knuckles went white gripping the edge of the armrest. The stewardess stopped to check on me.

"When will we get down?" I asked, my voice edged with desperation.

"Not long. We're just circling," she replied. "Here's another bag."

"You mean we're there?" I asked.

"That's right. But we can't get down because of the cloud cover. We need a break in it."

"And if we don't find a break?"

"It's back to Halifax."

"But Halifax was really foggy when we left."

"Then it's on to Stephenville."

"I'll never make it alive," I groaned.

"Sure you will," replied the stewardess with conviction. "We haven't lost anyone yet."

"My Uncle Phil is waiting for me in Sydney, not Halifax."

"Keep your fingers crossed then," she said.

I leaned back into the seat in pure misery. The airsickness bag waited. My whole world had been compressed into the space between me and the seat in front of me. I no longer cared whether the plane landed back in Ottawa, in Cape Breton or on an ice floe, as long as it came down out of the air. A red light went on. It said, "Fasten your seatbelts." That little red sign had come on many times since we left Halifax—about a hundred, or that's what it felt like. I prayed that this would be the last and fastened my belt once more. My ears began to pop. I looked out of the porthole. Thin wisps of cloud whipped by the window. I couldn't see any sign of the ground, but we were going down—I could feel it. Then, suddenly there it was. The familiar green of trees, a road, two or three lakes. I leaned back into my seat and hung on. It would soon be over. Individual trees began to emerge from the green. The plane banked slightly. There was the airport. The tarmac rushed up. The plane touched down, bounced once, the engines roared and we were safely on the ground. I reached for the airsickness bag and threw up for the last time.

"Welcome to Cape Breton," announced the pilot.

A chill sea wind had me shivering and shaking as I walked across the pavement to the little building. My legs felt as if they were made of rubber, but it was wonderful to be on the ground again. The airport certainly wasn't very large; it looked more like a big garage. Uncle Phil didn't seem to be here. I recalled that he looked a good deal like my Dad so I figured I'd recognize him, even though I hadn't seen him in a while. He shouldn't have any trouble recognizing me, I thought. I was the only boy in the airport. My bag came in on the little conveyor belt. I pulled it off and sat down on top of it. Then I saw him. He looked just as I remembered him, except more rumpled and he hadn't shaved.

"Boy, am I glad to see you, Uncle Phil." The words just burst out.

"Clive. It's good to see you too. Are you okay?"

"Sure, I'm fine."

"Where did you sleep, last night?" asked Uncle Phil.

"In the airport at Halifax. What about you?"

"I didn't. They kept announcing your flight was going to be arriving, and then two minutes later they'd cancel it. So I just stayed put. Have you had lunch?"

I shook my head.

"Would you like to get a bite to eat before we go?"

"No thanks."

"Let me take your bag. It's going to pull your arm off."

Uncle Phil picked up my huge suitcase. It certainly was good to see him. Maybe the summer wasn't going to turn out so badly after all.

"Sure you don't want to stop for something to eat?" asked Uncle Phil again. You look pale."

"I couldn't eat. I'll wait with you though if you want to eat."

"No, I'm okay," replied Uncle Phil. "Perhaps by the time we get to Baddeck your stomach will have settled down a bit."

"I hope so." I opened the car door, lowered my head and slid in along the front seat. No doubt about it, I was feeling better with every minute. Still shaky, but that terrible heaving in my insides had settled down to a distant rumble. Uncle Phil started the engine and we were off. We drove in silence for a time until we reached the outskirts of Sydney. It didn't take long until we were rolling along the highway.

"When will we see the ocean?" I asked.

"When we get to Margaree Harbour," replied Uncle Phil. "In about an hour and a half."

I was disappointed. I had figured that since Cape

Breton was an island, the ocean would be immediately visible, especially since one of the few things I could remember clearly from my visit as a little boy was standing by the sea with my sand bucket and shovel. What I hadn't figured on was the size of the island.

"How are your Mom and Dad?" asked Uncle Phil.

"Just fine," I replied.

"And your sisters?"

"They're fine too."

"Is Lydia still as blonde and petite as ever?"

"Yes," I said.

"Now, *she's* a Doucet," said Uncle Phil. "You and Anna are too tall and dark—not unsightly mind you," grinned Uncle Phil. "Just too tall, too dark and too many freckles."

I didn't respond. It was an old family joke. Anna and I look like Olivers, my mother's family, and Lydia was growing exactly in the style of the Doucets, small, fine-boned and very blonde. It was a bit of a sore point. While Lydia swanned off to ballet lessons, I was constantly in deep trouble for gross clumsiness with an ingrained habit of breaking things. My own bones, assorted pieces of sports equipment and household furniture were all victims of my ineptness. Lydia was also very clever in school.

"What's the matter?" asked Uncle Phil.

"Nothing."

"When a kid says 'nothing,' it usually means 'something.' Remember, I'm a school teacher. Come on, out with it. You'll get no peace until you do."

"Oh, I have to repeat grade eight," I said, the words jerking out.

"So you repeat one year. Lots of kids have to repeat a year. It doesn't matter."

"It doesn't?"

That was not my father's line. He couldn't understand

it. I could see him now looking at my report card like it was a bad dream and if he looked hard enough it would go away.

"My father never failed any grade," I said.

"So that's your father, not you. It took me about five years to do a three year B.A."

"How come?"

"I took a year off off to work in a garage in the village. Another year, I travelled some."

"But, you didn't fail?"

"No, but maybe I would have if I had been at school. Missing a year isn't the end of the world. Sometimes parents let these things get out of perspective."

"Can I roll the window down, Uncle Phil?"

"Feeling sick?"

"No, I feel great. I just want to see better."

"Sure, roll it down."

"Is that the ocean?"

"That's the Bras d'or lakes," said Uncle Phil. "We cross them over there. See the bridge. Baddeck's not far on the other side. Think you'll be able to eat by then?"

"Maybe just a cup of tea," I replied, still mistrustful of my stomach. We stopped in Baddek. Uncle Phil had a coffee and I had some tea.

"How much further to go?"

"Down the Margaree Valley, then up the coast to Grand Etang."

"I sure will be glad to get there. How much longer will it take? Does Grandpa have horses?"

"About an hour and, yes, he does have horses. As well as some cows, sheep, chickens and a couple of pigs the last time I looked."

"Neat-o."

"More like 'work-o'," smiled Uncle Phil and we headed down the Margaree Valley. I began to watch for signs that said Grand Etang or St. Joseph du Moine, which was the name of the parish. But I was to be disappointed. There were plenty of Margarees—South West Margaree, North East Margaree, Margaree Forks—but nothing that said Grand Etang or even looked remotely French. Everything was Scottish.

I couldn't remember what Grandpa's farm looked like so I tried to imagine it from the little black and white photographs I had seen in our family album . . . a white frame, two-storey house, some gables, clapboard. It could have been any one of the farms that we raced toward and then past. I didn't even know if the house was beside a river . . . near the highway . . . up on a mountainside . . . or on the outskirts of this village called Grand Etang. What was the village like? Was it a cluster of houses near a fork in the road? I thought it might be. The Margaree Valley didn't look much different from home.

One photograph did remain clear in my mind. I was about three years old, sitting in something called a buggy, with a small whip in my hand, my mother holding on to me. Sometimes I wondered if that little figure was really me. It was a good deal better being twelve, I thought. You could do so much more. A chill shook me, goose bumps patterning my arm.

"Almost there," said Uncle Phil, pulling me out of my half-sleep.

He slowed the car down as we approached a long, narrow wooden bridge which crossed the mouth of the Margaree River. I was conscious of the highway rising abruptly on the other side and suddenly we could see the ocean stretching out before us. The effect was electric—the height of land, the green mountains on the right, the grey ocean spilling out forever under the blue sky . . . a glimpse of the neverending openness of the universe. It was as if someone had suddenly tipped me close to the edge of space.

I looked about for trees, to get the walled valley feeling

I was used to, but I looked in vain. The fields spread back in long, neat rectangles toward the distant mountains. It looked so cold, so exposed, not inviting at all. It would take time, but I was to learn that this magnificent sense of space and open horizons wasn't something to fear, but to love. And once you came to love it, it became a limiting feature of the mind by which all other environments were measured.

"Uncle Phil?"

"Yes?"

"Could you tell me when we can see Grandpa's?"

"Sure."

"Is Grandpa's farm in the village?"

Uncle Phil cocked his head a bit to one side as if considering a problem of some magnitude.

"It's a bit difficult to explain, Clive. Why don't you wait till we get there?"

"Why is it so hard?" I asked, puzzled.

"Well, Grand Etang is the name for the harbour and the area right around it—the fish plant, the Co-op store, the fishermen's houses. Your grandfather lives about a mile from the Co-op in St. Joseph du Moine parish."

"So Grandpa lives in St. Joseph du Moine the parish, but not in the village of Grand Etang," I interrupted, anxious to impress Uncle Phil with my quick grasp of the obvious.

"Not exactly. You see, the provincial highway department here put up signs—now when was it? Oh, I guess it was just after the war. . . ." He stopped talking and a slow smile spread across his face.

"Yes?" I asked.

"Well, they put up signs from one end of the parish to the other and you know what they said?"

"St. Joseph du Moine?"

"No, Grand Etang."

"How come?"

"Because when the roads superintendent from the highway department stopped at the Co-op and asked the manager what the name of the place was, he was told 'Grand Etang,' which was, of course, what it was. No one thought much of it at the time. Except six months later we had 'Grand Etang' plastered from one end of the parish to the other."

"So where does Grandpa live?" I asked, still confused.

"There's considerable debate about that and has been ever since the signs went up," smiled Uncle Phil again. "Some say Grand Etang. Some say St. Joseph du Moine. Some say both. Generally visitors refer to the parish as Grand Etang because the post office is down at the harbour. But I think you'll find Grandpa and most of the farmers regard themselves as being from 'du Moine.' " At that point my uncle broke into great heaving guffaws of laughter. He sounded just like my Dad. The car swerved a bit and Uncle Phil slowed the car until the laughter subsided. "Don't worry about it, Clive. It doesn't really matter. Grand Etang. St. Joseph du Moine. We know where we are, even if the rest of the world isn't sure."

"Why doesn't someone write to the highways department to explain the mistake?"

"And spoil all the fun? Well, here we are. See, over there . . . the big farm below the hill?"

"Yes, I see it. Gosh, is it ever big. Is it Grandpa's?"

"No. That farm belongs to the parents of your Aunt Marie-Hélène. See that barn and the big truck in front? That's your Uncle Gerard's."

"Does he have any kids?"

"Two—a boy and a girl. The boy's about your age. See that little house? That's your Great-Uncle Felix's."

"What's his name?"

"Who? Gerard's boy?

"Yes."

"Roland."

This long list of relatives that I was acquiring so quickly was all a bit bewildering. I had no idea that so many people were connected to me. I half wondered if Dad knew.

"You wanted to see where your grandfather's farm is?"

"Yes, please."

"There it is." Uncle Phil pointed across the fields to a small, white clapboard house. It seemed a long way back from the highway. He turned the car in between two trim fence posts and suddenly we were crunching down the farm's gravel road. I felt a knot of excitement in my stomach. Everything was so new, so different from the city life I was accustomed to. We stopped at the side of the house in front of the porch.

"We're home," said Uncle Phil with considerable relief in his voice. "Ah, it's a long drive. I'm stiff. Let's go inside. I followed Uncle Phil up the porch steps and through an inside porch.

"Be back in a minute," he said, and disappeared through one of the doors. I was left in what I guessed was the kitchen. Although it wasn't like anything I had seen at home. It was a very large room with light spilling in through two windows. Wooden tongue-and-groove strips acted like a kind of skirt around the walls and above this skirt the walls were painted white. The kitchen table was small and set on casters so that it could be moved around easily. The stove, or what I guessed to be the stove, had truly grand proportions, taking up almost all of one wall. There were six round burners on the top, a large plate warmer above, a hot water tank at one side of the oven and the fire box at the other. I found a closet tucked beside the stove that discreetly stored the wood. The rocking chair beside the stove must have been Grandfather's. Along one side of the room there was a row of hard-backed chairs. A simple, wooden crucifix hung on the wall. A counter ran from the edge of the kitchen sink along the entire length of that wall with a neat row of cupboards below and above it. The refrigerator looked as it did at home, modern, white and stuck in a corner. Above it, on a shelf, was a large collection of coal oil lamps. All in all, without people, it was a bright but utilitarian room. Only the doors leading off to other parts of the house betrayed the kitchen for what it was—the heart of the house. Uncle Phil re-entered.

"No one home. Let's take your bag upstairs."

"Is that the stove?" I asked.

"Yes, most people keep their wood stoves here."

"How come? Can't they get electric ones?"

"Sure, but there's lot of wood around, and they warm the house when the electricity fails, which it sometimes does in winter."

"Do you own one?"

"Both electric and wood."

I followed my uncle through one of the doors leading out of the kitchen past the dining room and the front room where the television stood in magnificent splendour, upstairs to my bedroom. It was a small room at the end of the hall. The ceiling sloped upwards on one side. A large double bed was set at one end of the room, a chest of drawers at the other. From the window you could see the line of the sea coast and the sea beyond. Uncle Phil dropped the suitcase on the bed and sat down beside it with a contented sigh. He bounced on the mattress a couple of times.

Just as hard as ever. You know who used to sleep here? Three of us! Armand, your dad, and me. And now look . . . one small boy in one big bed. Ah well, times change!"

"Should I unpack?"

"No, leave it until Germaine gets back. She'll have her own idea about where everything goes anyway."

"Where is Aunt Germaine?"

"Out visiting, if I know your aunt."

"And Grandpa?"

"Let's go and find out." We left the suitcases on the bed and clattered back downstairs.

"When was the last time he saw me?"

"Who?"

"Grandpa."

"Wasn't it when your Dad was at St. Francis Xavier?"

"I guess so," I replied, not really sure, but the picture of the small child sitting on the buggy seat came back to me.

Uncle Phil strode across the polished linoleum floor of the kitchen downstairs towards the porch door. I followed him. Outside, the raw wind tugged at my jacket as we walked up to the top of the small hill that sheltered both the house and the barn.

"There he is. Can you see him, Clive?"

"No."

"Follow the line of the fence. See—the house and cart about half-way to the back pasture?"

"Oh yes, I can see. What's he doing?"

"Why don't you go and ask him?"

"Where are you going, Uncle Phil?"

"To the hospital in Chéticamp to see if you have another cousin yet."

"Oh," I said, remembering Aunt Catherine's condition.

"What's your preference? A boy or a girl?"

"Doesn't matter," I replied, and then remembering to quote my mother, "as long as it's healthy."

"Well, we should know soon," said Uncle Phil with a smile and he almost ran down the hill to his car. "See you later," he called and I watched the car circle the house in a spray of gravel. The big sedan swayed back down the lane towards the highway like some land-bound ship and I was left wondering about the uncertainties of navigating the final distance between me and my grandfather.

It didn't look very promising—there were a lot of monsters between me and Grandfather. I wondered if cows were violent. They certainly looked violent. They were big and had horns. I thrust my hands deep into my trouser pockets and walked toward the fence. Best to look nonchalant. They wouldn't be concerned if I acted nonchalant. Maybe I should wait. But how long would I have to wait? No, that was a cowardly strategy. I climbed up to the top of the gate ready to go over. One of the distant cows raised its large horned head and gazed my way. Suddenly I wasn't so sure. Didn't only bulls have horns?

"Grandpa! Grandpa!" I called, but the sound of my voice evaporated into the air somewhere between the spring daisies and the sea breeze. It was as if I had said nothing. The field flowers nodded their heads in agreement. Grandpa would never hear me. I jumped down into the field. The brown and white cow lowered her head. White-knuckled, I gripped the top of the gate and flung myself back over the fence. I landed with a crunch on the other side, shaken but still in one piece. The animal that had just threatened me so dangerously was now placidly munching grass. So much for my fears. With a hammering heart I climbed back over the fence and began to walk up the slight incline of the field towards Grandpa, but I stayed as far away from the horned animals as possible—just in case. The cart grew in size. As I approached, it became clear that it was really quite a large vehicle. It had two wooden wheels, both taller than I. Grandfather stood inside the cart. He was holding a large steel mallet. A short, wiry man, his face was sun and wind burned to a deep, rich mahogany. He wore steel-rimmed spectacles perched across a sharp, thin nose. He was slim, dressed simply in faded jeans and a checked shirt that was crossed by wide suspenders. He looked ageless, neither old nor young. He laid the mallet down as I approached, and at the same time pushed a cloth cap back from his forehead. A curly lock of snow-white hair escaped.

"Hello, Grandpa," I said.

"You must be Clive."

"Yes."

"Did you have a good trip?"

"Yes."

"Very good, would you like to climb up?"

"Yes."

"Then come round the front. Don't worry about the mare. She won't kick."

"Gosh, is she ever big."

"Fair size. Here, give me your hand."

I climbed up on the shaft, a little nervous until I realized the horse couldn't kick me even if she wanted. I gripped Grandfather's hand and he swung me over the side boards. I had arrived.

The bottom of the cart held a number of fence posts, some coils of wire, and an open wooden tool box. Grandfather pulled a large pocket watch out of his trousers and examined the face.

"Are you hungry?" he asked, peering at me over the top of his steel-rimmed spectacles.

"A little," I said, surprised to find that I was.

"Good. We can finish these fence posts then. Have you ever driven a fence post before? I seem to recall your father was pretty good at it."

"No."

"Would you like to try?"

"Sure."

"See that post?" he said, pointing to the one directly opposite us. "It's a new one. Has to be driven in like this," and he swung the sledge hammer above his head and brought it down with a solid crack squarely top of the fence post. It didn't look hard. Grandfather handed me the mallet. I grasped the handle as he passed it to me and immediately dropped it on my foot. The pain was excruciating. I screamed softly.

"Are you all right!"

"Yes," I gasped, the pain shooting up my leg.

"What happened?"

"It's just a bit heavier than I thought."

"Did you bring some boots?" asked Grandfather.

"No."

"Perhaps I had better finish the job."

"Boots aren't going to help me lift the hammer, Grandpa."

"I know but. . . ."

"I'd like to try. I think I can do it," and with gritted teeth and great determination I swung the mallet over my head as I had seen Grandfather do . . . but as I did the horse shifted her weight slightly from one foot to another. The cart moved a fraction under my feet. Grandfather ducked and I went flying over the edge of the box, still firmly gripping the mallet. God knows where I could have landed if Grandfather hadn't caught me by the seat of the pants and one leg. My flight was arrested and I came flopping back to the side of the cart, suspended upside down, my hands sweeping the grass, the mallet resting a good fifteen feet past the fence line. It wasn't as easy as it looked.

"Ça va, mon petit?" enquired Grandfather delicately.

"Pardon?"

"Do you speak French?"

"Sure."

"Like you swing a mallet?"

"Kind of," I said as Grandfather let me slide to the ground.

"Then I think we'd better speak English," said Grandpa as I hit the ground. I gazed back up at him from my comfortable position in the grass.

"Mom says we have to speak French."

Mon dieu. It's going to be a long summer. How about you and I speak French, but when we're in the house we speak English. Then when you get the hang of it, we'll try French with your aunt? Kind of surprise, O.K.?"

"O.K."

"Clive?"

"Oui, monsieur?"

"Your shirt is ripped."

"I must have caught it on something.

"I would guess so," answered Grandfather with just the shadow of a smile playing at the corners of his mouth. "Would you pass the mallet back up here?"

"Oui, monsieur," and I crawled under the fence to fetch the mallet.

"Let's go back to the house," said Grandfather, "while you're still in one piece."

"What about the new posts?" I asked.

"They can wait until tomorrow. You need a rest."

"I can do it," I protested. "I just need some practice."

"And you'll get it tomorrow, lad," said Grandpa smiling. "There's plenty of time." Grandpa sat down on a small wooden seat fastened to the front of the cart and snapped the reins across the rump of the horse. The huge animal wheeled like a pony and began to trot briskly back to the barn, leaving me behind calling, "Grandpa, Grandpa, wait for me."

The cart slowed and I scrambled to get on. After several clumsy attempts I managed to clamber up. *"Très bien,"* said Grandpa. It was to be the start of a wonderful relationship, but at that moment I had other things on my mind like hanging on, as the springless box cart bounced over the rough field. I tried to imitate Grandfather's casual style—one foot forward on the broad, wooden shaft, the other back, braced against the box. I settled for a death grip, holding on with both hands. I was still more or less erect when the horse stopped with a jerk at the barnyard gate whereupon I flipped neatly backwards into the bottom of the cart, tearing the knee of my new trousers as I tumbled.

"Clive?"

"Oui, Grandpa."

"*Ça va?*"

"I'm fine."

"Are you sure you didn't cut yourself on the barbed wire?"

"No, no, I'm fine," I repeated stubbornly, refusing the temptation to glance down at my knee. But Grandfather remained unconvinced.

"You'd better get up to the house and get changed."

"Why?"

"Because Germaine will have my hide if she sees your clothes like that. She's very fussy about appearances and right now yours are way below standard."

"Couldn't I stay and help unharness the horse?"

"It's not a horse. It's a she and her name is Nellie. There will be other days, like tomorrow. Now get going. *Vas-y!* Or I'm in deep trouble."

"Yes, Grandpa," and off I went, anxious to do something right. I was a good runner and I sprinted across the barnyard. But it was not to be my day. Unschooled in the topography of barnyards, my headlong dash had not taken me very far before my right foot squished into what felt like mud but wasn't. I slithered wildly, my right leg flailing away for solid ground. For a second it looked as though the coup de grace was imminent, but somehow I kept my balance, although I had the distinct impression the horse was laughing. I kept my back resolutely in her direction and limped the rest of the way across the yard, this time more careful in tracing my trajectory.

On gaining the hill which overlooked the house, I decided to take my damp shoe and sock off. I wiped my shoe on the grass as best I could, learning as I did it another important fact about the properties of fresh cow dung—it clings. I soon had the viscous, distinctly smelly stuff on my hands, shirt sleeves and trousers. It was a bit like bubble gum, green bubble gum, green, smelly bubble gum. I hobbled the remaining distance to the farmhouse. Grandpa was right. I was a mess—torn trousers, one shoe off and one shoe on, a bruise on my cheek. I opened the porch door but before I could enter the inside porch Aunt Germaine met me. She was a thin, rather excitable lady. She took one long look at me before uttering something between a screech, a scream and my name.

"Clive, don't move! Take those clothes off right there!"

"Pardon?"

"You're not coming into my house with half the barn. Shirt, trousers, socks, shoes—off! Leave them on the railing and then go straight upstairs for a bath!"

"Yes, Aunt." I stripped under her critical eye, the sea breeze seeming a good deal cooler than I had formerly noticed. Aunt Germaine then shepherded me upstairs to the bathtub, all the time talking a blue streak.

"How was your trip? How's your Dad? Your Mom? Do your sisters still wear dresses or are they wearing slacks? Did they like the scarves I sent at Christmas? I've put your clothes away. Your shirts are in the top drawer, trousers in the second." As she talked the hot water roasted my legs red. The steam from the bath misted the window. I listened and watched as Aunt Germaine added some soap flakes to the hot water. "And don't forget to clean the tub when you're finished. The cloth is under the sink."

"Yes, Aunt," and she left as the soapy bubbles rose in a silvery honeycomb under my nose. Grandpa was right. He was going to get skinned alive.

The merry crackle of the wood stove greeted my entrance into the kitchen. The room was baking-bread warm with the aroma of dinner all around. Aunt Germaine smiled at me and said, "Now that's more like the boy I remember."

Grandfather sat in his rocking chair by the stove, one leg cocked comfortably over the arm of the chair. His skin looked definitely in one piece but I noticed his boots were parked by the door and on his feet he wore store-bought moccasins. He winked, a short twinkle that Aunt Germaine did not catch. I smiled back at him, but my eyes returned to the kitchen table. It was piled high with all manner of good things—golden brown bread, oven biscuits, fresh butter. The china basin stood steaming. I wondered what it was filled with. On the counter were bowls of freshly-sliced bananas and thick, whipped cream.

"Supper is ready," called Aunt Germaine. Grandfather and I wasted no time. We sat down at the table, Grandfather at the end, Germaine and I on either side.

"I wonder if Uncle Phil has had his baby yet?" ventured Grandpa.

"If he has, I want to hear about it," said Germaine. "I don't think it's ever been done before." She laughed and so did Grandfather.

"Have you ever had *fricot*?" asked Aunt Germaine as she ladled out a steaming spoonful of thick soup from the china basin into my bowl.

"No."

"That's funny. I thought your father would have cooked it."

"What's in it?" I asked, stirring the heavy soup around. I had said the wrong thing. Aunt Germaine hadn't said anything but I could feel it. "It smells delicious," I said, trying to regain lost ground. "Mmmm, and it tastes even better." And it did.

"That's good," said my aunt, mollified. Then, remembering my question, she said briefly, "*Fricot* is a potato and chicken soup."

Grandfather watched the exchange between us and I had the distinct impression he was smiling, although outwardly he remained impassive. I was learning. Inside the house it was Aunt Germaine's territory and what she said, went. Grandpa kept his peace.

The *fricot* was good and as the warm soup filled my stomach I began to realize how very tired I was. Even the spoon felt heavy. It was difficult to believe it was only six o'clock and that I had left Ottawa that very morning. It felt like a week ago. I watched Grandfather take a thick slice of bread with his dessert. "Would you like some bread with your dessert?" asked my aunt.

"Yes, please," I responded cautiously. If bread and butter tasted fine with soup, why wouldn't it taste good with the bananas and cream?

"How do you like the cream?" asked Grandfather. "It's from our cows."

"It's delicious," I replied, but I wondered how the cow gave whipped cream.

"Pardon me for a moment," said Grandfather, and he stood up to turn on the radio. "I just want to get the weather for tomorrow."

"You're looking very pale, Clive. Is there something wrong?" asked Aunt Germaine.

"I am a bit tired."

"It's the air down here," said Grandfather. "It takes a while to get used to."

"How do you know, Papa?" teased Germaine. "You've never lived anyplace else!"

"Because that's what people tell me," smiled Grandfather.

"Who?" she asked.

"The tourists."

"Sure," doubted my aunt.

"You watch. Tomorrow Clive will come with me when we go to the store. He'll tell you it's true." I wondered what Grandfather meant but didn't have the chance to ask him.

"Would you like some more dessert, Clive?" asked Aunt Germaine.

"I think if I eat anymore, I'll burst."

"Ah-ha. So that stomach of yours does have a bottom. Would you like to watch some television?"

"Can I help with the dishes?"

"Now, isn't that polite," approved my aunt with a beaming smile.

"No, not tonight. You go and watch the T.V."

I coasted gratefully out of the warm kitchen and into the front room. The T.V. eyed me from the corner. I turned it on. A French channel. An English channel—*Dragnet!* A good show, but somehow I couldn't seem to get interested. The heavy supper, the long day, the gentle motion of the rocking chair, a kettle boiling in the background. I started to nod off.

"Clive. Clive." Aunt Germaine's voice came from far away. "Do you want some tea?"

"No thanks."

"You don't have to stay up. Do as you wish. The bed's free."

"Maybe I will go to bed."

"I must say I'm surprised. I thought all teenagers watched television until one o'clock in the morning. I've been preparing myself for it all week."

"I'm not a teenager yet."

"Weren't you thirteen in March?"

"Twelve."

"Twelve. That's a good age," said Grandfather as he entered the living room quietly in his moccasins. "Not too old, not too young. When I was twelve I used to work for old Doctor Fiset."

"What did you do?"

"Oh, carried drugs and the like by horseback. Sometimes I even assisted at operations."

"When you were twelve?"

"There was no one else," shrugged Grandfather.

"What did you do?"

"I held the chloroform over the patient's nose, washed up, helped with preparations."

"Gosh, no twelve-year-old would be allowed to do that now," I exclaimed.

"Those times were different," said Grandfather. "I didn't go to school."

"Can I get up with you in the morning, Grandpa?"

"*Bien sûr.* Listen for the crackling of the stove. That will tell you I'm up."

"Good night, Grandpa. Good night, Aunt Germaine."

"*Bonne nuit,* Clive."

I climbed the stairs a little shamefacedly. What would my friends back in Ottawa think if they knew I was going to bed at seven o'clock! It was just the time for baseball down at the park, not sleeping. But they weren't around to see me and anyway I didn't care. I was tired and I was going to sleep. As Grandfather said, tomorrow would be time enough. Tomorrow was a new day and I wanted to get up early with Grandpa. He got up at six o'clock. I had never been up that early before in my life. Nor had I ever milked a cow. . . .

From under the eiderdown I listened to the evening breeze knocking gently at the windowpanes. It sure was different at Grandpa Doucet's. The wild openness of the countryside, the stretch of sea under the sky—it was exciting, as if I had entered a new world. And best of all I belonged. I wondered if Grandpa would let me ride a horse . . . soon I was dreaming of falling out of planes in a cloudless sky.

First Day

For a few moments I wasn't sure where I was—the sloping ceilings, the big four-poster bed—and then I remembered ... Grandfather's! I listened for the stove and couldn't hear a thing. All was quiet. I dozed for a while. The morning sun reflected below the curtains. I wondered vaguely what time it was ... six o'clock? I threw back the covers and was immediately struck by a rush of cold air. I went to the window, shivering slightly. Yes, it was all still there—the neat fields stretching down to the sea and that meant I was still here. I dressed as quickly as I could and, carrying my shoes in my hand, tip-toed downstairs. I pushed the kitchen door open gently. Grandfather was standing at the kitchen stove. The room was cosy and warm; the delicious smell of frying bacon was in the air. Grandfather looked up from stirring an open pan of porridge.

"Clive, what took you so long? Half the day is gone."

"Are you finished milking?"

"Long ago." Grandpa pointed to the four bright dairy buckets sitting on the counter. "But you're in time for breakfast."

"Oh," I said disappointedly. "I wanted to try."

"You'll have to get an alarm clock or listen better to the old rooster."

Disappointed, I walked over to look at the four gleaming dairy buckets. They were much larger than normal buckets—and they were empty. "You were joking!"

"Yes, I was. Come, sit down. We'll have breakfast and then we'll do the milking. A man can't work on an empty stomach."

Grandfather ladled out two great heaping bowls of porridge, then poured a generous helping of cream over the porridge, followed by a sprinkling of dark brown sugar. It was delicious. I had a second bowl and then we started on our second course—thick strips of home-cured bacon, fresh eggs, toast, strawberry preserves and tea. We ate in pleasant silence, the crackling of the wood stove keeping us company.

When we had finished breakfast Grandfather stood up as if he had just had a light snack, his thin frame betraying no sign of anything more than coffee and toast. I waddled to the door after him.

Grandfather laced on his boots and I, my shoes. Outside the sun had crested on the highlands and sunlight was spilling across the high pastures, lighting the land in soft colours. It was a glorious feeling to be right in at the start of a new day. I wondered why I had never done it before, but Grandfather was already disappearing towards the barn. I ran to catch up to him, my milk buckets clanking together in the still morning air.

I pushed the small door open and stepped onto the wooden threshing floor. In the belly of the barn the cows stood below us patiently waiting. We went down a small, narrow flight of stairs to the stable. The air was heavy with the sweet smell of hay. A ginger cat perched expectantly on a rafter. Grandfather gave me a small wooden milking bench.

"There isn't much to it," said Grandfather as he sat down beside a tall, yellow-brown cow and rested the milk bucket expertly between his crossed legs and the floor. He pulled on a teat and a jet of milk hit the bottom of the pail with a surprisingly loud crack. It did look easy. "Why don't you try the Ayrshire? She's quiet."

"Which one is the Ayrshire?"

"The brown and white one at the end."

"Are you sure she won't mind?" I asked as the brown and white cow eyeballed me with a great rolling, violet stare.

"She doesn't usually, but if you're worried, tie her leg."

"Does she kick?"

"She will if you pinch her teat," said Grandfather nonchalantly. "Let's tie her leg for now, just to be on the safe side. Rope? Rope? Where did I leave that cord? Here it is."

He reached up to a peg where several small coils of hemp hung. A small loop was made in which he slipped her right hind leg. The other end he snugged down to a heavy staple driven into the timber floor for that purpose.

"There you go. You're safe. She's fastened fore and aft."

I nodded brightly and sat down on the stool about six feet from the cow. But it's difficult to milk by long distance. I edged closer and closer until my forehead was inches from her flank. I noted with surprise that she didn't smell bad at all; in fact, kind of pleasant. Unfortunately there was no way I could communicate this good news to my colleague. I took a deep breath and grasped the cow by both her teats. She did not stir. I pulled first one and then the other. Nothing happened. The cow went on munching hay. I pulled a little harder. A short dribble of milk ran down my fingers. Success . . . well, sort of. I tried the left hand. This time it took all my strength to bring the milk down. Then I tried alternating as Grandfather was doing—left hand, right hand, left hand, right hand. The barn rang with the sound of morning milking. I was so proud. Although my contribution that morning was a meagre one, Grandfather was obliged to finish the brown and white cow for me as I found my forearms were tired to the point of being unable to use my fingers long before the cow's large udder was empty. Still I felt a proprietary sense of achievement as we placed the last warm bucket onto the shelf for safekeeping.

Grandfather pushed the doors open and the morning sun came pouring into the barn. "They should go up to the high pasture this morning. Will you open the stanchions?"

"Sure," I replied, but before I could say more, Grandfather had disappeared out the doorway and I was left to puzzle the eternal question: What are the stanchions? There didn't seem to be any lying around on the ground. Surely Grandfather had meant me to free the cows and that must mean the stanchions must secure them in some way, which implied the stanchions were located at the front of the cows, rather than the back. I proceeded to the front of the smallest cow with authority. Two upright wooden poles went up and down each side of the cow's neck, allowing her to feed easily but preventing her from withdrawing her head from the manger. A small hinged board held one of the poles in place. Obviously the hinged board must be the stanchion. If I lifted it, the right pole could fall to one side and the cow would easily be able to back her head and horns out of the stall. It seemed an easy chore, except that if I freed the cow in the tight confines of the stable, she would then be able to gore me at her leisure—unless I climbed onto the top of the beam into which the stanchion was fastened. It would be safe to release the cow from there. I proceeded to do just that. Once safely sprawled along the beam, I flipped the board up. The pole slid sideways and the little yellow cow placidly backed out of the stall without even a curious glance in my direction. A piece of cake! The next two I boldly freed from the side, their great horns almost brushing my chest as they backed out, until only my cow—the brown and white one—remained. Perhaps she was angry at me for my clumsy milking efforts. I decided that until we got to know each other a little better, discretion was the better part of valour. I climbed up onto the beam and released her from there. She too made straight for the stable door until her back leg hit the end of the rope Grandfather had tied down for my safety, whereupon she was transformed immediately into a bawling and kicking monster. "Stand still!" I called. She didn't listen. Damn. Why hadn't I remembered the rope? The strength of the cow was awesome. The floor timbers the iron staple was secured to creaked and groaned as she lurched powerfully. I was amazed at her desperation. "Stand still," I shouted again. The cow didn't understand my request and the rope held. What was I to do? Unless she stopped thrusting with her hind leg, the animal would surely dislocate her hip. Forgetting my fears, I scrambled down from my perch, calling, "Whoa, Bossie. Whoa." But the sound of my voice did not soothe her. If anything she seemed to redouble her efforts, her huge udder jerking back and forth and the heavy rope flying like string. I bent over the rope, helpless. The knot that fastened the rope to the staple was pulled wire tight. There was no way anyone could undo it. Nor did the heavy staple show any sign of coming loose. The cow's bawling reached a screaming pitch. I could feel bubbles of sheer terror breaking out in bits of prickly heat over my face. Damn! Couldn't I do anything right?

Grandfather appeared in the doorway. Without speaking, he pulled a small, sharp pocket knife out of his trousers and cut the rope with three swift strokes, timing the last so that the brown and white cow did not stumble when she came free. Bewildered and still bawling, the cow staggered out the barn door. Grandfather tipped his old peaked cap back on his forehead and smiled at me, a clear twinkle in his eyes. "No damage done, Grandson. It could have been worse." I nodded, too relieved to find words.

By some lucky miracle the cow's convulsions had not rocked the open cupboard where the fresh pails of milk sat. Grandfather picked up one pail in each hand and, balancing one in front and one behind, he climbed the narrow stairs to the threshing floor. I picked up the remaining two. It was surprising how heavy the milk pails were. The dead weight of the dairy buckets pulled my arms straight. But once a few steps up the narrow stairs, I was obliged to pull one bucket higher than the step in front. It had to be done with the flex of a single bicep. I flexed. Nothing happened. I flexed again, straining with all my might and stepped upwards. The bottom of the bucket caught on the edge of the stair and some warm milk spread over my knee. I wasn't going to make it. The old slugger himself could not lift one ordinary milk bucket up one lousy stair. With a terrific effort, I wrenched the buckets up the final four stairs. By the time I reached the top, the weight of the bucket in front was no longer a serious problem. Half of the milk was distributed over the stairs and over me. So much for terrific efforts. Next time I would carry one at a time and use two hands. I poured some milk from the full bucket into the half-empty one. The cats followed me, purring appreciatively and I followed Grandfather down the hill towards the house. As I entered the house I noticed the sun was now in a more recognizable place in the sky. It looked and felt more like morning. At the inside porch door Grandfather had carefully taken off his boots and slipped on his moccasins. I took off my shoes and entered Aunt Germaine's sanctum in my stocking feet. I wondered if she would be up. She was. Using both hands, I carefully put my pails on the counter beside Grandfather's.

"*Bonjour, Tante*," I said.

"Good morning to you, Clive. Would you like some tea?"

"Yes, please."

"Come closer, Clive. What on earth have you done to your jeans?"

"I spilled a little milk."

"About half a gallon, I'd say," said Germaine dryly. "Go change them, right now I'll not have you dripping all over my clean floor."

"Yes, Aunt." I skedaddled out the kitchen door and up the stairs, somewhat offended. I wasn't dripping . . . much.

When I returned Grandfather was operating the strangest-looking machine. It was set up in the corner of the kitchen—a large aluminum bowl on top, two spouts below and out of each spout shot a jet of milk.

"What's that?" I asked Grandfather.

"A cream separator. It separates the cream from the milk."

"Why do you want to separate it?"

"We sell the cream to the dairy."

"What about the skim milk?"

"The calves drink it."

"You have calves."

"Yes. They usually come with the milk."

"Can I see them?"

"Of course. Take a bucket and we're on our way." This time I took just one bucket. "Be careful," warned Grandfather. "That's the cream."

I looked down at the dark yellow substance and lifted it very carefully. This stuff was sold for money. Again I followed Grandfather, treading as if I were walking on egg shells. We reached a well close by the house without incident. Several large aluminum cans sat in the cold water at the bottom of the well. Grandfather lifted one of them up. I passed him the bucket and he poured the fresh cream into the large container.

"Keeps the cream cool," said Grandfather as he lowered the can back down into the well. "The dairy truck only comes twice a week and if it's not fresh, you don't get paid."

"Did you ever not get paid, Grandpa?"

"No, the cream always stays fresh down there."

"I see. It's kind of like a big outdoor refrigerator."

"I hadn't thought of it quite that way, but you're right. That's what it is. What else? Oh, yes. We're going to have to get you some farm clothes before you go banging about in the barn. Otherwise it's going to be a continuing war between you and Germaine."

"Why?"

"Well, she has some set ideas about what good clothes should look like and yours don't fit that image. In the first place you can't go tramping around in those shoes. Can't figure why your father sent you down without boots. We should go to the store and pick you up some."

"How?" I didn't see any car.

"See that red shed at the side of the barn?"

"Yes."

"There are two buggies in there. Pull the one on the right out. I'll feed the calves and be round in a minute with Nellie." Grandfather disappeared through the small barn door, swinging the pails expertly beside him. It was a bit of a blow to be left out of feeding the calves. But the "buggy" had a certain attraction. The shed Grandfather had pointed to was a long, sloping affair, one end attached to the barn. At the other end two wide carriage doors were held shut by a large wooden pin and a long pole propped against a block and then thrust against the door. It seemed a rather primitive arrangement. I pulled up the stick that was pressed against the doors and the block. Then I tried to knock the pin free, but it wouldn't budge. Freeing the pole had caused the two doors to settle forward tight against the pin, binding it. Another mistake. I fought to get the pole back in its original position, pressed between the block and the door. But the pin remained jammed. This is ridiculous, I thought. I can't even open a damn door. I pushed as hard as I could on the pin but the big doors still refused to move. They remained jammed tight against the pin. In a fury I picked up a rock and tried to hammer the hardwood pin loose. I cut my finger. "Calm down," I told myself. I was not totally incompetent. I sucked the cut on my finger and tried to console myself. I was a passable hockey player, the best football player on my block. There must be a trick to it. If I was to lay the butt end of the stick against the block and ease the other end of the pole down, down, down against the door like it was before, the weight should lift off the pin and come into the pole. Putting theory into practice was another thing, though. I pushed down on the pole until my face went red. The long, heavy doors creaked, creaked again, and to my great joy the door moved back up on its hinges . . . not much, but just enough to take the weight off the wretched pin. I kicked the small end of the pin with my heel. It shot clear of the clasps easy as pie. Next step. Lift the pole up. Both doors swung open to the grass.

My eyes strained to adjust from the sunlight to the dim light of the shed. There were the two buggies, parked side by side in the shed. Above, perched on the rafters were two sleighs, one a heavy box sled made from rough wood, the other looking like it had been taken out of a Christmas card. I'd better stop gawking. Grandfather had said to get the buggy. I planted myself firmly between the shafts of the buggy on the right and lunged forward into the sunlight. The buggy moved so easily behind me I came close to ending up on my face. Once outside I could see why. Unlike the springless cart, it was built with both grace and speed in mind—four wheels with delicate, finely turned spokes neatly pegged into a thin rim, a single upholstered seat sitting on steel springs, a small trunk at the back, a whip slanted by the driver's side. The whole effect was altogether pleasing. This vehicle was obviously designed for better things than the cart.

I had visions of Grandfather and me on the way to the store, speeding down the highway, passing cars. Then Nellie, harnessed and ready to go, clip-clopped into sight and my visions disappeared. There was no doubt she certainly had a commanding presence—her great splayed hooves, huge neck, chest and belly. In fact, hugeness was her main asset, speed a distant second. I figured in a pinch she could probably outrun any angry cow. Nellie regarded me with a benign indifference. I wondered how Grandpa was going to get her hugeness between those two delicate shafts. It seemed an impossible task but obviously Nellie didn't perceive it the same way. Grandfather backed her up between the shafts, Nellie's great feet moving cautiously but steadily backward until she was parked neat as you please between the two slim poles. Then it was just a matter of lifting the shafts up and hitching Nellie to them. I looked at the odd pieces of leather on my side and tried to relate them to the metal fixtures in the shaft. I had figured out one piece when Grandfather came around to my side and finished the simple hitching for me. Seemed like I couldn't do anything but Grandfather smiled at me.

"Don't be disheartened, Clive. You'll learn. It's easy when you know how."

I was to become quite familiar with that phrase over the next few months. We climbed into the buggy, the small seat rocking on its springs as we did so. Grandfather snapped the reins and with a tremendous fart, Nellie moved off. This large, ebullient sound repeated it-

self at regular intervals and was accompanied by a vigor-
ous outpouring of horse balls as we clip-clopped down
the lane to the highway. Once we turned onto the main
road, the eruptions began to subside.

"Isn't Nellie a bit fat," I suggested delicately to
Grandpa. He cocked his head to one side as if actually
considering this priceless piece of wisdom.

"She is a bit fat," he acknowledged. "She's also old. Believe it or not, she used to be a pretty speedy little thing. I
can remember when we had to keep her on light machinery because she just wasn't steady enough for the
mower or the hay wagon."

"How old is Nellie?"

"About twenty."

"That doesn't sound old."

"Makes her about seventy in our years."

"Oh," I said.

"And she's in foal. That doesn't help."

"What's that?"

"She's going to have a small one—a colt or a filly."

A colt or a filly! I watched the fat old girl clip-clopping
along, her belly taking on a new importance in my mind.
"That's fantastic! When? I hope it's before I go home."

"It should be sometime in late August."

"Yippee. I'll be here. How far is the store?"

"Just down by the twist in the highway."

"It's not too far for her?"

"No," said Grandpa dryly. "I think she'll make it."

The road went straight as an arrow down the edge of
the sea coast, a neat line of houses and barns on the right
side facing the road and the sea. I couldn't see the store
but the curve was clear enough—not much more than
half a mile. Grandfather snapped the reins and the mare
increased her pace. Clip clop, clip clop was exactly how
her steps sounded. I could see the store now.

The Co-op didn't look like any store that I had seen before. It was a long, low building that, except for the sign, looked more like a warehouse. The front was painted white but the sides remained a weathered clapboard grey, just like the fishing sheds down by the harbour. The front doorway was set in between two plate glass windows and above the doorway on a western-style false front was written "Co-op" in blue. Grandfather guided the mare across the highway. The buggy wheels crunched onto the gravel. Beside the store were several short posts with iron rings set into the top. Grandfather tied Nellie to one of the rings and we walked into the store.

Inside, the Co-op looked a bit more like a store, but not much. The aisles seemed to go everywhere. There didn't seem to be any order to the displays at all. There was no painting done inside. The rafters were exposed. It should have felt cold, but it didn't—and the low lighting, the dark wood, the piles of goods combined to give it a dense, intimate atmosphere. Scary. I stuck close to Grandfather. He joked with the manager. I tried to follow the conversation in French, but the men were speaking so quickly I couldn't. Grandfather pushed me forward and I was introduced to Monsieur Calixte Doucet. *"Clive à Fernand, à William."* Clive, the son of Fernand, the son of William. The manager's head was completely bald. We shook hands, my hand disappearing inside his large, rough hand. Everyone in Grand Etang seemed to have oversized hands.

Then we all marched over to the shoe section. No sign indicated shoes but the pile of rubber boots, hip waders and leather boots stacked, racked and hanging made it clear where we were. Shoes didn't seem to be a big selling item down here. The manager wore boots; Grandfather wore boots. My own feet looked kind of naked in their city shoes. There were two wooden chairs for sitting in and a small stool in front of me. I sat down. The manager pulled several pairs of boots down off the rack and then called, "Anne! Anne!" A girl looked up from behind the cash and then came over. She looked about fifteen, kind of an embarrasing age difference—too old to be friendly with, but not old enough to be an adult. She said, "Hello." I nodded. We didn't shake hands. She was very pretty. I swallowed, unable to take my eyes off her but unable to speak. She handed me two pairs of brown leather boots. I tried the second pair on with a heavy pair of socks that she gave me. A shaky walk followed. The boots felt stiff and clumsy and they squeaked. "They seem fine," I mumbled. I couldn't tell if the girl was laughing at me. The whole thing was very embarrassing. I wanted to leave the store in the worst way but Grandfather shepherded me down another aisle, this one piled with clothes.

"Coveralls and a rough jacket," said Grandpa briefly to Anne. The girl nodded and Grandfather walked over to another section of the store. The thin girl looked at me, sizing me up like some small calf while I squirmed inside. She pulled several pairs down from the high counter. "These should fit."

Mercifully, before we could pursue the matter further, the bell over the door jangled and Anne left to serve the new customer. I breathed a great sigh of relief. Safely hidden inside a plywood changing room, I pulled the coveralls on. They looked ridiculous but the length fitted. The heavy plaid jacket had a bit more style but not much.

Grandfather was waiting for me by the checkout counter when I finally arrived with my packages. His were already neatly packaged up in brown paper. Anne smiled at me. I felt my face flushing deep shades of pink, but no one seemed to notice. Grandfather paid the bill and then Anne helped us carry the packages to the buggy. We packed them carefully in the trunk. I was surprised at how little room there was. Sure was different from a car. We put the jeans and boots under the seat. Grandfather climbed into the cab while I untied the reins from the hitching post, but as soon as he was seated Nellie deftly wheeled and began trotting towards the highway.

"Wait! Wait for me, Grandpa."

"Hop on."

I glanced at the small gap between the two revolving steel wheels. The step was no bigger than the sole of my boot. Grandfather slowed the mare's pace. I jumped, catching the step properly but the forward motion of my jump caused me to shoot violently into the cab. The delicate buggy swayed dangerously, threatened to tip and then righted itself.

"It's easy when you know how," I said before Grandfather could. He grinned.

"How did you like our store?"

"It was O.K. The girl, Anne, seemed kind of young to be working there."

"Let's see now ... Levi Chiasson's youngest daughter ... must be almost sixteen. That reminds me, I should drop in and see about getting Donald."

"Who's Donald?"

"An old horse of mine I loaned to Levi for his spring ploughing."

"How many horses do you have, Grandpa?" A sudden vision of a frolicking equine herd appeared before my eyes.

"Two."

"Oh," I said disappointed.

"Unless you've got a very big farm, two horses are plenty. This isn't the prairies," smiled Grandfather.

"Dad said you used to keep more."

"Well, I used to keep stallions."

"Stallions? That's really something. What were their names?"

"There was Prince. He was a big, black Percheron.

Strongest horse I've ever seen. And then Donald, a Clydesdale-Hack cross. I think Donald was about the best stud we ever had—very gentle—but a big horse with good speed. He was a favourite of all the children. His mother died in foal and we had to raise him by hand."

"Is the Donald that Mr. Chiasson's got the same horse?"

"Yes. He's an old fellow now and no longer a stallion."

"How come?"

"Not enough work. Everyone was switching to tractors. There wasn't any reason to keep a stallion. But I can remember a time when most of the foals from Inverness to Cape North were either out of Prince or Donald. And fine foals they were, too. There's Levi's."

"Where?"

"Up there." Grandfather pointed east toward the mountains. I looked but still couldn't see a thing. We crested a small rise and then I saw it—a very small house perched right under the mountains.

"It's a long way off."

"Yes, it is. Used to be a lot of houses up on the high pastures. Not many left now."

"Why aren't there?"

"Too much trouble. It's far from the road in winter."

"Why does Levi stay there?"

"He has a big family."

"How many?"

"Six children. These days it's not easy to find a house for six children."

"Does he have any boys about my age?"

"At least one."

"What does Levi do?"

"He farms, does some carpentry work, works at the fish plant—a little bit of everything."

"How does he farm without a horse?"

"He has Donald most of the time. I only need him for haying and the odd trip to the mill. I use a team very

rarely now." While we were talking Nellie had slowed
down to a fast crawl. Then Grandpa's hands telegraphed
something along the leather reins and she picked up her
pace once more.

"When will we go?"

"Where?"

"Up to Mr. Chiasson's?"

"Too late now," said Grandfather glancing at his
watch. "This afternoon there will be time enough."

After lunch I helped Aunt Germaine with the dishes
while Grandfather retired to his rocking chair by the
warm stove. He tipped the chair easily back onto its long
rockers which extended about three feet behind the chair
and then in a comfortable, semi-horizontal position he
quickly dropped off to sleep. I didn't realize it then, but I
was looking at an antique version of the giant lazy boy
chair which would soon sweep through the rec-rooms of
North America at $300 a crack. At that moment, though,
my mind was on other things; specifically, how could we
get up to see Anne's place? The tiny house nestled under
the shadow of the mountains intrigued me and besides I
was anxious to see the famous Donald.

"Aunt Germaine?"

"Yes, Clive."

"When do you think Grandpa is going to wake up?"

"In about half an hour."

"Are you sure?"

"He always does. Why?"

"Well, we're supposed to go up to Monsieur Chiasson's
to pick up Donald this afternoon."

"Don't worry. There will be time enough. Grandpa
always has a nap after lunch. Why don't you take one? It's
good for the digestion."

"But I'm not tired."

"Try lying down on the couch. It's a long day when
you're up at six."

"Really, Aunt Germaine, I'm not tired."

"Take a book with you then," and she gently but firmly shuttled me into the living room. Somewhat irritated, I picked out a book from the small bookcase. Inside the cover was written my Uncle Armand's name. It looked a little like a school book. I laid down on the couch to begin reading it. The early afternoon sun played lazily across the room. I must have fallen into a profound sleep, for the next thing I remembered was someone persistently shaking my foot and calling me from a great distance.

"Clive. Clive. Wake up, sleepy head. It's almost one-thirty."

"One-thirty?"

"Yes," said Grandfather. "Don't you think we'd better get going?"

"Yes, yes, I'm ready." I groggily flipped my legs off the couch and unsteadily stood on my feet. They felt foreign and far away. I couldn't believe it. I had been out like a light for over an hour. Sheepishly I avoided Aunt Germaine's amused gaze as I shuffled across the shiny, linoleum floor. It wouldn't do to slip and fall on my behind. I laced on my new boots, all the while feeling my aunt's eyes on the back of my neck.

"Feel better, Clive?" asked Aunt Germaine brightly as I looked up. Better admit it, I thought.

"Yes, I do. Guess you were right—but at home naps are only for kids."

"I see," she said gravely. I left the house unsure whether my aunt was laughing at me or sympathizing. She was difficult to figure out.

Outside, Grandpa was waiting for me in the buggy. I swung onto the seat beside him and off we went. Nellie seemed to have benefitted from her lunch break too. She moved at a smart pace down the lane.

"Grandpa, how come Aunt Germaine never got married?"

"Pardon? I can't hear," shouted Grandfather. So I shouted back at him so that my voice would carry over the racket of the steel-rimmed buggy wheels banging and grating against the gravel.

"How come Aunt Germaine never got married? I think she's pretty!"

"Too fussy, I guess," said Grandpa jokingly.

"What do you mean?"

"Well you know how fussy she is about the house— everything must be always spotless. Well, she was the same way about men."

"She wanted them spotless?" I asked. Grandfather laughed.

"Exactly. She was very choosy, one day the choices ran out."

"I see," I said. But I didn't really. For a while the noise of the buggy was our only company. Then Grandfather spoke in such a low voice I wasn't quite sure I had heard him right.

"No. It's not quite that simple, Clive. No, I shouldn't joke about it . . . You should know, Clive . . . But today is too beautiful for sad stories." He said nothing more and I did not press him. Nor did I want to. We continued on our way until we came to the long, grassy lane that led up to Monsieur Chiasson's place.

The lane was absolutely quiet. Our buggy wheels made no sound against the grass. From the embankment on either side of us, wildflowers dropped down. Behind the fencing, sheep and cattle grazed. We were moving along under a great ocean sky, surrounded by the soft scents of the deep countryside. It all seemed a bit unreal to me, as if we were inside a picture someone had painted. I could distinguish no details, no distinctive smells, no sounds, no sights. The tranquillity weighed upon me like a stone. Surely a car would suddenly overtake us. I fidgeted.

"Grandpa?"

"Yes, Clive."

"Could I try driving Nellie?"

"Do you think you can handle the traffic?"

"What traffic?"

"Rabbits," said Grandfather in a tone that was dead serious.

"Rabbits?"

"Sure, Nellie is a skittish creature. See the blinders on the bridle? Poor old girl doesn't know her age. She'll jump at a butterfly."

"What would you do if she bolts?"

"Hold on, I guess," Grandfather laughed. "Draw the reins in steady but surely, and talk to her until she quiets down." Grandpa handed the reins to me. As soon as the lines were in my hands Nellie slowed from her brisk trot to a slow walk. Grandpa pretended not to notice our change in pace. I slapped the reins across Nellie's rump as I had seen Grandpa do. She farted and proceeded at the same leisurely pace.

"Grandpa?"

"Yes, Clive."

"How do the Chiassons get to their place? In a buggy like us?"

"Sometimes, but mostly they use their car."

"On this lane?!"

"No. They come by the back way."

"Which way is that?"

"There's a parish road at the back. It runs just below the high pastures, then dips down around the pond."

"Where's the pond?"

"You can't see it from here. But see how Levi's house seems to be right up under the mountains?"

"Yes."

"Well, it's not. There's a sharp drop—about a half mile behind Levi's to a saltwater pond. The mountains that seem to begin from just behind Levi's house really begin on the other side of the pond." I examined the country in front of us looking for the gap between pasture and mountain which hid the pond. There was a sort of cut but it looked like the natural line between field and forest slopes. The forest side seemed to start steeply, that was all, but perhaps that was the giveaway. Meanwhile, as I had been examining the mountains ahead, Nellie's leisurely walk had slowed to a meander.

"Mind if I drive now?" asked Grandpa politely. Somewhat reluctantly, I handed the reins across to him. Grandfather gathered the lines and as he did so, Nellie's head came up from her pleasant discourse with the grassy bank. With a mouthful of grass still firmly clasped between her teeth, she was off, her legs once again swinging rhythmically along as if to say, "It wasn't me, boss!" I watched Grandfather's hands. They remained steady, moving slightly and rhythmically to accommodate the movements of the mare's head, in contrast to my flailing hands which had alternated between irritating Nellie and ignoring her. The trick was obviously in the hands, not in the voice or whip. I resolved to do better the next time— if there was another one.

When I looked up from my deliberations on the art of horsemanship we were almost at Anne's house. Like Grandpa's, the Chiassons' house was tucked under the shelter of a hill, except the hill around their house was higher than at Grandpa's. It came right up to the roof line on every side but the one facing the sea. When you were up close to it, it seemed almost buried in the hillside. A neat little gabled place, though smaller than Grandpa's house and not painted at all. The clapboard had been washed by the wind and rain the same slate grey colour as the barn. I had never seen a house without paint before but it didn't look out of place. The sheltering hill, the soft grey colour, made the little house blend into the landscape in a natural and comfortable way.

In front of the house, surrounded by a strong fence to keep browsing cows out, stretched the largest garden I had ever seen. At the far end Mrs. Chiasson bent over some plants, two small children weeding and playing beside her. "Levi's probably in the barn," said Grandfather, breaking me from my thoughts. "You coming, Clive?"

"Are you going to be long?"

"Shouldn't be."

"I'll wait then."

"As you wish." Grandfather waved to Mrs. Chiasson and set off towards the barn. I remained in the buggy. It felt neat, holding the reins by myself, master of all I surveyed, which was considerable. From my high seat I had a view of the hay fields rolling down towards the sea and then the infinite, curving surfaces of the blue sea and sky meeting far beyond. There was a sense of spaciousness and wonderful possibility to the moment that I had never felt before. It was a grand feeling that words can only poorly convey.

Suddenly I jackknifed straight backwards, the reins flying from my hands. Nellie was off like a shot from a cannon. She veered crazily to the right and then crashed into the fence, stopping abruptly. This time I was flung violently forward and I made what was beginning to be a familiar arc through the air before striking the ground with a thud. The landing knocked the wind clear out of me and I lay gasping for a few moments like a fish out of water. The pain was momentary but quite excruciating. I lay still and tried to shut out the picture of the brown rabbit bouncing across the garden. It didn't work. The rabbit remained; so did our elegant buggy, tilted on its side, one wheel spinning in the air. Nellie didn't move. Her leg seemed to be caught in the barbed wire. My breath started to come back, along with a rush of pure guilt. Why me? Why couldn't I do anything right? Why hadn't I tied her up? A face loomed over mine—a soft feminine face.

"Comment vas-tu?"

"I'm fine."

"Are you sure?" She slipped an arm under my shoulder and helped me to my feet. "No bones broken?"

"I don't think so."

"Come into the house with me. You look very pale."

"What about the buggy?"

"It's not going anywhere," said Mrs. Chiasson, regarding the spinning wheel with a wry smile.

"That's what I'm afraid of." I limped over to look at the mare. Her leg was caught in the fencing but she didn't seem to be in any pain. Then I noticed blood dripping down the back of her trapped leg. She had cut it on the barbed wire. I grasped the edge of her bridle and began to talk to her as I had seen Grandfather do. Her leg trembled a little but remained still. I couldn't tell if the cut was deep or not. Someone had to get her leg out from the wire. If Nellie moved suddenly again, she would cut it more. I grasped the fetlock as I had seen Grandfather do and gently pulled. Nellie seemed to understand the nature of her predicament for she raised her hoof carefully, following the gentle pressure of my hands exactly so that both knee and great splayed hoof were guided through the upper and lower barbed wires.

"Nicely done, Clive." I turned and saw Grandfather. "Are you all right?"

"Yes, I'm O.K."

"May I take a look?" Grandpa bent down and folded the edges of the cut neatly back. "Hmm. Nothing serious. A wash with some salt water and a tetanus shot will fix her up."

"Are you sure she'll be O.K.?"

"As sure as the sun is shining. I'll wash the cut out. It won't take long. Could you get me a little iodine paint from the barn?"

"Yes, Grandpa."

"Oh, before you go . . . was it a rabbit?"

"Yes, I'm pretty sure it was."

"Crazy old lady," growled Grandpa at the rotund mare. Nellie hung her head, her soft, grey muzzle almost resting on Grandpa's shoulders.

I set off for the barn, a large, low, grey structure behind and to the right of the house. Its unpainted walls didn't give off the prosperous appearance of our own red and white barn but the building had a farm look about it. There were hens pecking away at the grass, ignoring two huge cats which were sunning themselves lazily on the grass. I headed for the main doors which stood ajar. A wagon of a type I hadn't seen before was parked in the bay. Suddenly a boy about my size emerged from the shadows of the central doors. He was leading a giant chestnut horse. The boy nodded to me as he approached.

"I'm looking for the iodine," I said, not knowing quite how to introduce myself.

"Bottom shelf on the right," said the boy, indicating the stable door with a brief wave of his hand.

"Thank-you," I replied but he had already continued on his way leaving me to find the iodine. It was exactly where he had said it was but for the first time, I felt a little lonely. It would be nice to have a friend my own age.

That evening I went down to the small pasture which abutted the ocean side of the barn. It was a rough, hummocky little piece of land that zig-zagged along the edge of the farm—a useless field for hay or cultivation of any kind, but it served perfectly as an outdoor stable. There was a clear, deep spring at each end, as well as a cool summer shed which was used for calving. Generally it was used for any animals that Grandpa wanted to keep handy to the house without confining them to the barn. This rough land was fenced into three sections: a night pasture for the milk cows so that we didn't have to make a long trip in the morning to fetch them; a section fenced off for cows near calving; and another for the horses, which was why I was there that evening. I couldn't get over the chestnut horse, Donald, his reddish-gold coat glowing in the late evening sun. Four white feet, a blaze down his face. Poor old Nellie. She seemed like such a humble creature beside him—shorter, brown and round; that was Nellie.

I wondered what it would be like to ride the chestnut horse. Would Grandpa ever let me?

"What are you thinking about, Clive?" I jumped. I had been concentrating so hard, I hadn't heard Grandfather approach.

"I was wondering what we were going to use Donald for?"

"Oh, I imagine we'll find something," smiled Grandfather.

"Like what?" I asked, unable to contain my curiosity.

"Well, I'd better pick up some timber Gerard cut for me last winter. It's a chore I've been putting off. After that, I think we'll give Nellie more rest than she's been getting."

"Because of the foal?"

"Yes."

"What about the Chiassons?"

"They'll use a tractor for their haying."

"Oh."

"Don't you think that's a good idea?"

"Sure."

"You don't sound too sure."

"Well, Anne's brother didn't say much to me. He seemed kind of mad at me."

"Maybe Joe was shy. Did you speak French?"

"Yes. When do you think I will see him again?"

"Probably on Sunday." Grandfather looked at the little garden which lay between us and the house. "Ugh!"

"What's the matter?"

"How I hate gardening!"

"Why?"

"Oh, I don't know. Something about the hoe, I guess. Never liked working with a hoe. Too picky. But your grandmother loved gardening. For her it was a great relaxation."

We began to walk back towards the house, the sun spilling its last fiery glow across the sea's horizon.

"In the summer she would often sit out here in a lawn chair and watch the sunsets," said Grandfather. "I can't ever see a sunset without thinking of her.

I didn't say anything because I was afraid. I lowered my head and pretended I didn't see the tears.

Sundays

Sunday morning. I felt my stomach tighten with the usual combination of fright and boredom. Church always did that to me. Nothing new, except that it seemed slightly worse. I sat in the small rocker by the radio pretending to read, trying to ignore the fact that I was dressed in my best trousers, shirt and stiff leather shoes that squeaked when I walked. Sunday morning hymns were coming out of the radio and I turned it off. No one protested. Aunt Germaine was upstairs putting the final touches on her Sunday morning outfit. Grandpa sat lost in thought in his rocking chair by the stove. He looked like a different person. Gone were the jeans and yesterday's stubble. He wore a dark suit with a double-breasted jacket, white shirt and polished black shoes, which replaced his old brown boots. His face was smoothly shaved and his white hair brushed correctly. Only the deep outdoor tan gave him away for what he was, a farmer.

No doubt about it, I was nervous. Soon I would meet some of my cousins and maybe Joe Chiasson. My insides tightened down a notch further. I didn't want to go. But there was no escaping it. To miss mass was a mortal sin. Only a real fever could pry us away from that Sunday morning obligation. I would have to go.

We waited for Uncle Phil to arrive. He normally drove Grandpa and Aunt Germaine to church in his car, although we could easily have gone by horse and buggy because the church was only two miles from the farm. But in 1959 it wasn't considered appropriate to use a horse and buggy on Sunday; hence the chauffeured occasion. (Neither Grandfather nor Aunt Germaine drove a car.) So we waited, all the while my nervousness growing.

It is a pre-requisite of the Roman Catholic religion that anyone marrying outside the Church must swear to raise his or her children within the Catholic fold. It is an oath that has soured many marriages and many children on religion. But for devout Catholics there is little choice— the penalty for disobeying is excommunication. My father took the oath and my mother, for love of him, agreed.

Father was, and is, a man of his word. Each Sunday morning he faithfully escorted his three children to church. We attended to our catechism and when we reached the age of seven or eight we were all dutifully confirmed.

I wasn't old enough to understand; I only knew I didn't like watching my mother go to another church each Sunday. I didn't like the draughty ceilings and bundles of people sitting in long rows enduring the ceremony. Better to endure than feel guilty. Better to divide and conquer. That seemed to be the sum total of the religious experience. I didn't give a hoot for it, convinced the fine words the priest spoke cloaked a great deal of mindless cruelty—as Mother had made sure part of our education around confirmation time included instruction in the religious wars. The Spanish Inquisition was not forgotten. Not that I was anxious to become a Protestant. I just wanted out. But twelve-year-olds aren't allowed that kind of luxury, or they weren't in my family. I kept my sentiments to myself. There was no point in protesting and I didn't bother trying.

Uncle Phil arrived and we all climbed soberly into the back seat of his car. I was wedged firmly between Grand-

father and Aunt Germaine. Someone was already seated
next to Uncle Phil. No one introduced me and Sunday
morning wasn't the time to ask impertinent questions.

A few minutes later, Uncle Phil turned into the church
yard. Grandpa got out rather stiffly in his Sunday
clothes, and sauntered over to talk to some friends who
were clustered down by the road. I set out alone; my one
thought was to get it over with and I headed straight for
the church door. Aunt Germaine walked towards the
back of the church, and Uncle Phil said, "Bye, bye."

"Where you going?" I chirped at him, a little desperate
at the idea of being left alone with all these strange people.

"Home. I went to the early morning mass."

"Oh," I said. "How will we get home?"

"I don't know. Dad just asked for a drive one way. See
you later." And Uncle Phil waved cheerily and departed.
I looked at my watch—10:25. Mass was to start in five
minutes. Why wasn't anyone inside? Maybe I had got the
time wrong.

"Clive?" I turned gratefully at the sound of my name
and there was Joe Chiasson standing in front of me, a big
grin on his face.

"Hi," I said.

"Hi," said Joe. "May I introduce you to a cousin of
yours? Roland Doucet meet Clive Doucet," and Joe's grin
grew even bigger. Roland looked to be about ten. We
shook hands. I had never met a cousin before. Roland
was a good deal more practiced than I was because he
broke the impasse easily.

"Doing anything after mass, Clive?"

"No, I don't think so."

"Then why don't you come to my place for dinner?
You and Joe." And before either of us could answer, Roland said, "See you later," and took off for the back of the
church.

"Where's he going?" I asked Joe.

"I guess he's serving mass."

"Oh . . . are you coming for dinner at Roland's?"

"I'll go and ask my parents," said Joe, and I was left to search out Grandfather as the church bell began to ring. In answer people began to make their way slowly towards the church door. Where was Grandpa? Already inside, I guessed. But no. There he was. "Grandpa! Grandpa! Wait for me. Grandpa, I just met Roland. You know . . . my cousin! And he asked me if I could go over to his place for dinner. Can I?" Grandpa looked at the man beside him and smiled.

"What do you think, Gerard? I'll recommend him. He's a good eater."

Uncle Gerard cocked his head to one side as if really considering the matter but there was no time for a response. We had finally made our way inside the church door.

The ritual began. I crossed myself with practiced authority, genuflected and followed Grandpa down the outer aisle towards our pew. A few seconds later, Aunt Germaine joined us. There was an uncomfortable rustling and thumping as people found their seats. The altar boys entered. I recognized Roland, his collar slightly askew. Then the priest. We all stood to celebrate mass. I knew every word of the litany off by heart in Latin. The comfort of familiar ritual. The idea of mass being comforting immediately struck me as novel. In my wildest imaginings I had never before thought I would find mass comforting.

I tried to look around the church without seeming like a tourist. My father had been an altar boy here. He had studied for his provincial exams with the help of the parish priest, Father DeCoste. I had heard all about Father DeCoste. A saint, a veritable saint. He visited the old and lonely. He was one of the founders of the coopera-

tive movement in Inverness that eventually liberated fishermen and farmers alike from the tyranny of exorbitant
interest rates and constant debt. Without Father DeCoste
there would have been no parish library and without the
library, few boys from the parish would have successfully
negotiated the provincial exams. An able and honest man
whose spirit lingered on. After his death some of the
young men he had helped got together at St. Francis
Xavier and wrote an essay in his honour. They had pub-
lished it, too. We had a copy at our house in Ottawa. I
had often leafed through it.

I knew all about Father DeCoste. That old priest, this
little church were at the root of much of our family misery. The funny thing was that once you were here, it
didn't seem possible. The building wasn't much larger
than a house. The structure was entirely made of wood.
The pews were more like benches. The statuettes were
humble plaster of paris. The bellowing of the choir interrupted further reflection. It sounded like someone was in
pain. What a *mêlée* of competing octaves! Unashamedly I
craned my neck to get a better view of the blast but it was
not possible. A sturdy post blocked my view.

The priest was a short fellow with a firm but pronounced belly. Surprisingly, though, he had a deep, resonant voice that filled the little church with rich tones. He
needed no microphone. And when his voice joined with
the choir, he seemed to almost lift them by main force
into tune. But his sermon seemed out of character. No
fire. No brimstone. No purgatory. I can't recall what he
said at all, only that he spoke French clearly and easily,
but with a decided English accent. Nobody seemed to
care, which made me think that perhaps I was being
overly self-conscious about my own language abilities.
The sermon ended. Communion began. I breathed a
sigh of relief. Not too much longer to go. Wrong again.
To my astonishment almost the entire congregation par-

ticipated in the communion ceremony. My principal re-
action to this phenomenon was, my God, with only one
priest it is going to take forever!

Such was my faith or lack thereof. I waited for the final
blessing, the sign of the cross. We genuflected for the last
time and filed out of the church, heads slightly bowed.
Duty done for another week.

It never occurred to me that a few hours later I would
be pitching a baseball at the short, fat priest while his
great voice would boom towards me from behind home
plate, "Way to throw, kid. Way to throw. Right on down
the line."

Grandfather's seemed to have an endless number of
places to explore. My favourite in the house was a place
called the eaves bedroom. It was a tiny room tucked
under the eaves of the house. At one time, it had actually
been someone's bedroom. A small bed was still lodged
under the window between the edge of the house and the
slope of the roof. But it hadn't been used as a bedroom
for years. It was a very private place, tucked away from
the mainstream of the house. The inside of the room had
the same sort of shape as a large tent. It was a perfect
place to while away a rainy afternoon. The room was cluttered with trunks and boxes. Inside each box, sometimes
carefully packed, sometimes jumbled, were laden the
treasures of many childhoods. Books, toys, letters. There
were old-fashioned pictures and games, clothes, a picture
of my Dad with a guitar, standing beside two other young
men, one with a fiddle and the other with a guitar. He
looked very young, not much more than a kid. I had
never thought of my father as a kid before.

The first level of my grandfather's attic was easily as
magical as Kubla Khan's cave. It was there, not in any
classroom, that I learned to read French and it was there

I began to have the first glimpses of the kind of child-hood my father had lived through. For a long time, I didn't venture up to the second level, which was by way of a ladder to a small crawl space located just below the peak of the roof. I didn't bother going up because I reasoned there probably wasn't much of interest up there. In reality, it was because mice terrified me and there were mice living in the crawl space. Sometimes I could hear them squeaking around at night. I was afraid that I might put my hand on one as I transferred from the ladder to the crawl space floor. Then sheer terror would either drive me right straight through the roof or I would fall back down the ladder. Neither was a very pleasing prospect, so I contented myself with reading *Les Trois Mousquetaires* and the like from the safety of my sturdy ship, the old bed.

My favourite book was an obscure, dog-eared French title called *Le Capitaine de St. Onge.* I have forgotten who it was written by but I remember the story to this day. It wasn't exactly a children's story, although I suppose it was written for children because the hero was a boy about my age named Marcel. The story began on his father's small estate in the Gascony region of France. The family wasn't very rich and Marcel's father was often away from home. He was a *capitaine* in one of the king's cavalry regiments. From this position he obtained money and favours although the exact nature of the favours was never made clear. It was in one of *Le Capitaine's* prolonged absences that a greedy and powerful baron claimed Marcel's family's small estate as his own. The baron's soldiers arrogantly posted proclamations in the village which announced the baron as the new *seigneur.* The people didn't like it much but until the *capitaine* got back from the crusades to defend himself, there wasn't much they could do about it. They paid their taxes and kept quiet, all of which was pretty standard fare. Nothing to get excited about even if it did take a bit longer to read in French. Soon Marcel's father would return, the baron would be defeated and justice would be served. But it didn't happen quite that way.

The story took a bizarre twist in which it departed from the normal formula. It begins early one morning when some long-awaited mail arrives by courier. Marcel is the only one in the stable yard when the courier arrives. The boy recognizes his father's handwriting on the envelope, and excitedly he takes the package from the courier and rushes up the long, curving staircase to his mother's bedroom. He pushes open the heavy door to her bedroom unannounced and finds his mother attended by the evil baron. "They were in bed together." That is what the book said. *"Ils se couchent ensemble."* The evil baron and Marcel's beautiful mother.

My blood curdled. Marcel's mother screamed, and the baron swore, at which point Marcel finally unfroze and began running down the stairs. The baron was not far behind, still swearing. Marcel jumped onto the courier's horse which was still tethered in the yard and just managed to escape the last furious lunge of the baron. Marcel spent the night in the woods not far from the little château with the baron's dogs and soldiers prowling up and down the roads. There seemed only one solution, to find his father, which after many adventures Marcel finally did. His father was engaged with his regiment in the southwest corner of France near the Spanish border. It was a crusade against the Huguenots. But Marcel's success comes too late. He finds his father lying in a tent, dying from a fearful wound sustained in the siege. Marcel, seeing his father's desperate condition, says nothing of what has transpired at home, except to say all is well. *Le Capitaine de St. Onge* dies a few days later and young Marcel becomes a drummer boy in his father's old regiment.

From that point on the book was clouded with a vague sense of foreboding. Marcel still has many adventures. He even rescues a fair maiden from the clutches of some rapacious soldiers. She, of course, immediately falls in love with him. But Marcel pays her little attention. He is a cadet, intent on becoming an officer. But always behind his success you could feel he was just preparing himself for the final test—revenge. It was unnerving. Marcel was going to deny himself everything until wrongs had been righted. Yet the older he grew, the more difficult it was for me to figure out exactly what wrong had to be made right.

The time finally comes when the king offers Marcel a captaincy just like his father. Marcel refuses the honour and instead returns to Gascony. The people welcome him. The baron's rule has been an evil one. Men and women come willingly to Marcel's banner. They begin a resistance movement, operating from the mountains with clever raids on the baron's property until the old man is finally enticed out of his castle up into the mountains with the entire army to crush Marcel. Marcel's men are outnumbered and the peasants underequipped but, by pretending to retreat hastily, Marcel tricks the baron into entering a long, narrow valley high in the mountains. The baron's large army is forced to spread itself out in two's and three's all along the valley. His heavily equipped knights have no room to charge and use their lances. Finally, when the entire army is strung out like beads on a string, Marcel's bowmen, who have lined the wooded side of the valley, make short work of their targets. Marcel and a few men block the road at the far end of the valley, and the massacre is complete. Even the baron's fine armour fails him. He dies with an arrow in his throat. Marcel has won all but he refuses to enter the castle of the baron. Instead he becomes the guardian of the village church. From that moment on he never sang another song or rescued a fair maiden. He tended the flowers and swept the church floor. It seemed a perverse and scary story to me. Hadn't Marcel been a good man? Hadn't he been honest and fair? He deserved better. He had won. He had defeated the old ogre. He had avenged his father. The story troubled me more than I can tell. It didn't seem just. So I kept re-reading it, hoping to find something I had missed, something that would make sense of the puzzle; but I never did. (In fact I even began to see flaws in faithful old "Sir Ivanhoe." Why did he marry the rather insipid Rowena instead of the perky and brave Rebecca? Because Rebecca was a Jew? That didn't seem to make sense.) I didn't realize it at the time, but *Le Capitaine de St. Onge* was my last affair with romantic literature. I just stopped reading the stuff—but it was exciting while it lasted. I would have made a great knight.

The attic was a good place to daydream. When I wasn't with D'Artagnan, rescuing maidens from the claws of the lackeys of Cardinal Richelieu and the like, I liked to climb the mountain on the other side of the pond, a great mass of greenery that towered over the village; sometimes with gentle benevolence, sometimes with dreary fog. It was never quite clear what I would do once I reached the top. I had vague ideas of turning into an eagle and continuing on from there. Or maybe building a cabin and living alone. I would never have to go back to school. My specialty would be the non-school approach to living. Kids from all over the world would come to visit me to find out how I did it. Adults would be screened out by the invisible nature of my cabin and the orchard that surrounded it. Grown-ups would only see thick, impenetrable woods. This would be accomplished by a mechanism triggered by intentions. Any person who visited with the idea of proselytizing the virtues of school, and poof—no cabin, no orchard, just dense forest. Anne would be excused because I figured she had never been to school. A school with seven rooms didn't qualify as a school. At our friendly neighbourhood school in Ottawa we had more classrooms on one floor of one wing.

When I was reading or daydreaming, my eyes would often stray to the ladder that led up to the crawl space. It hung there in front of me, a constant reminder that basically I was afraid of tiny little mice. Eventually, I did muster up the courage to explore. Armed with a flashlight in one hand, the other firmly on the ladder, and a beating heart in the middle, I began to climb up towards the crawl space.

"You'd better run and hide, mice!" I called at the top of my voice. "You'd better run and hide! A big person is coming!" This, I figured, accompanied by suitable pauses and stern thumps against the ladder with the end of my flashlight, would frighten the mice into hiding. As the gap in the roof which led to the crawl space drew nearer, my pauses grew more frequent and my cries, louder. If only I could have entered the crawl space on my feet, I wouldn't have minded so much. But it was aptly named— you entered on all fours, or not at all. A vision of a dead mouse floating in the horse trough, its belly white and distended, appeared before my eyes. I took a step back down the ladder. I didn't really want to see what was up there anyway. "Would D'Artagnan have fled before a mouse?" I asked myself. It was hard to tell. He was always so busy duelling with foes. I wouldn't mind duelling with a foe myself. It was the idea of putting my hand on a mouse that was unnerving me. Only two more steps to go, Clive. Come on! I took the two steps. The beam from my flashlight pierced the sombre gloom of the crawl space and for an instant I caught the tiny figure of a field mouse scurrying along a beam. That definitely did it. I was not going in there. I swept the beam of light quickly once more across the space and illuminated three or four tin boxes. There didn't seem to be anything else in there. Just mice and a few tin boxes. I retreated back down the ladder in a composed fashion, my honour more or less intact. It was suppertime anyway and, after all, I had seen the place. Only one question remained—what was in those tins? Perhaps Grandpa would know.

The kitchen felt warm and welcoming after the sombre depths of the crawl space. I hurried to wash up as my aunt was already beginning to serve dinner.

"And what have you been up to?" asked Aunt Germaine as I pulled my seat up at the table.

"Do I look that guilty?"

"Small boys always look guilty," said Grandfather with a twinkle.

"I'm not small," I protested, quite affronted.

"That's true," said Aunt Germaine quickly. "Let me rephrase that for your grandfather. Boys always look guilty. What have you got to be guilty about?"

"Nothing much," I said.

"You didn't break anything?" she asked.

"No."

"Tear anything?"

"No."

"Fall on anything?"

"No."

"How disappointing," said Grandpa.

"Very unusual," said Aunt Germaine, trying to keep from smiling. "Have to keep up appearances, you know." I nodded, not sure whether Aunt Germaine was referring to the state of my clothes or the state of her smile.

"But I do have a question for you," I said.

"And what's that?" asked my aunt warily.

"Well, I climbed the ladder a little while ago to take a look in the crawl space just below the roof and I noticed some tins." Both Aunt Germaine and Grandpa began to smile broadly. "What's wrong?" I asked puzzled. "I didn't touch them."

"Wouldn't matter if you did," said Grandpa.

"Why?" I asked intrigued.

"Because of the mice," said Aunt Germaine. I jumped in spite of myself. "You've torn your jeans," exclaimed Aunt Germaine triumphantly.

"No, I haven't," I contested hotly, my dignity injured.

"Then why did you jump?"

"Mice. I don't like mice."

"Nor did Grandma," she said.

"What does Grandma have to do with it?" I asked, quite sidetracked from my indignation.

"Well," said Grandpa, "those tin boxes you saw are hers."

"What are they doing in the crawl space?" I asked, more confused than ever.

"Your Grandma was quite a baker," said Grandpa. "She especially loved to bake cookies—gingerbreads, date squares, oatmeal cookies, cinnamon rolls—but there was always a problem. The 'mice' would eat them almost as fast as she could bake them."

"In the kitchen?"

"Your father was one of those mice," said Grandpa, "as well as your Uncle Gerard and your Uncle Phil and your Aunt Germaine. We had about ten mice, as I recall, permanently installed in the kitchen."

"Oh," I smiled with relief. "But how did the tins get up there?"

"Well, one day after your Grandma had spent the better part of the day baking, she put the fresh cookies in tins and told me to put them up in the attic out of the way of the 'mice.' She wanted to save them for a 'do' she was having on Sunday. And that's what I did," said Grandpa with a smile. "I didn't even eat one and let me tell you that took some control because they smelled wonderful."

"But the tins are still up there."

"That's the other half of the mice story," said Grandpa with a smile. "When I went to get the tins on Sunday, the real mice had got into the tins and had demolished most of the biscuits. Well, you should have seen your grandmother when I told her. She was fit to be tied. All kinds of afternoon company and precious little to serve them. She was so disgusted she didn't even want to see the tins again. So I left them up there."

"Best thing that ever happened," said Aunt Germaine with a fond smile. "From then on there were no complaints when we ate too many biscuits."

Cows

During the spring and early summer the milk cows spent most of the daylight hours in the high pasture with the beef cattle. It wasn't a very convenient arrangement because it meant that each morning, after milking, someone had to drive them about a half mile up the back lane, opening and shutting a series of gates in order to see that they were safely pastured for the day. Then in the evening someone had to go and fetch the cows, but until the hay was cut, the milk cows had to stay in the high pasture during the day. We couldn't have them trampling our best hay fields, which abutted the barn. Once the hay was cut, matters could return to normal: the milk cows would graze in the fields closest to the barn, while the beef cattle and sheep would remain in the high pasture until the snow began. In the meantime there was this time-consuming chore of toing-and-froing with six, fat slow-moving milk cows. Grandpa was not keen on it, to say the least, but I was. It was an exciting evening when he let me go to the high pasture by myself.

We saddled Donald together and Grandpa checked the girth to make sure it was tight. Then out Donald and I went into the early evening sunlight. I suppose Donald looked rather foolish standing in the barnyard, a huge farm horse with a World War I artillery saddle perched on his broad back and a light riding bridle around his head. But to me he looked splendid—a gleaming chestnut charger, fit for a Knight of the Round Table. Now to get on him, that was Sir Lancelot's first problem. Not an easy task when the horse stands some seventeen hands tall and, try as I might, I couldn't quite insert my toe in the dangling stirrup. "Clive, use the sty," called Grandpa. I didn't understand what he meant so Grandpa came and led the patient Donald over to the little wooden steps which crossed the fence.

"You don't use them," I said, somewhat shamefacedly.

"Of course I do. It's the easiest way to mount a tall horse like Donald."

"Then how come I've never seen you use them?" I asked.

Grandpa pushed the tip of his cap back and scratched at his forehead. "Probably because I'm always in a hurry. When I was your age I didn't even bother with a saddle. Now up you go and don't hurry the cows home. They're not built for speed."

"O.K. I'll be careful . . . Grandpa?"

"Yes, Clive."

"I was wondering, what if the cows don't want to come home."

"What do you mean?"

"Well, we've got beef cattle up there as well as cows. How do I separate the cows from the steers? And what if the cows won't come?"

"Just get the old brown and white Ayrshire. She's the leader. The rest of the cows will follow once you have her. Don't worry about the steers. They won't be bothering about the barn until the snow flies."

"O.K.," I said somewhat cheered. It sounded easy enough. After all, the Ayrshire knew me. I had been milking her for over a week.

"Oh, Clive."

"Yes, Grandpa."

"If you want to gallop Donald, do it on the way up." I nodded grimly from my perch high on Donald's broad back. A fast walk would do me just fine but I wasn't about to admit it. Grandfather opened the barnyard gate and off we trundled. Donald ambled along at an amiable pace while I pretended that we were thundering down the home stretch at the Kentucky Derby. As we drew nearer the summer pasture gate, I gave Donald a couple of tentative prods with my heels. Donald bore them in good humour and we continued on our unhurried way. When we reached the summer pasture gate, I managed to slide off without breaking a leg. Then I tethered Donald to the fence. It seemed to be the most sensible thing to do, rather than have to worry about driving both horse and cattle through the gate, so I set off on foot to find the cows. I didn't have to go far. Both cattle and cows were gathered around the spring. The cattle paid me little heed, but several of the milk cows recognized the moment and began to plod through the buttercups toward the gate. I didn't see the old brown and white Ayrshire anywhere. There was another small hill just before the wood lot which Grandfather had kept to shade the cattle. I fervently hoped she wasn't in there because it was a sizable wooded area upwards of three or four acres and I had no idea how I would be able to extricate her.

But I was in luck, or so I thought. The old girl was parked just below the hill with a young steer standing tightly behind her, his two front legs spread across her back while his hind legs provided a rhythmic pumping action. It was a delicate and confused moment for me. In the first place, I wasn't quite sure if what I was seeing was what I was seeing. Secondly, if it was what I thought it was, I didn't want to interrupt anybody, especially not a ton of angry bull. My image of a bull was something big, reddish-brown and charging. He certainly filled the first two criteria and I didn't want to wait to test the third and so retired forthwith.

The cows were waiting for me by the gate. I unlatched

it and they all hurried through. Remounting Donald was all that remained to be accomplished. To my great astonishment, my first attempt worked. I had just enough of a toe-hold in the stirrup so that I could swing up and into the saddle. It was a wonderful feeling. Unfortunately, though, I found that once up on his back I was unable to untether the reins. With some despair and a few well-chosen words, I clambered back down and untied Donald. But once the reins were free I had another serious problem—the big horse wouldn't quite stand still. He shuffled, anxious to be heading back, while I engaged in a clumsy ballet—one foot in the air and one foot on the ground. After I had been dancing in this exhausting manner for some time, Donald finally gave up and stood perfectly still. I grabbed the pommel and with a fierce determination jumped, and heaved myself into the saddle, whereupon I swear the old horse breathed a sigh of relief. Back in the saddle again! The view was great and so was the feeling. Just then I heard a cow bawl and the Ayrshire came tripping over the hill. Her friend was nowhere in sight. My heart sank. Better to do it now than come back for her. I dismounted once more, opened the gate and she trotted briskly through. I carefully latched the gate after her, then Donald and I walked side by side back down the lane to the barn. Mission more or less accomplished.

"See," said Grandpa. "Down there at the head of the pond where the brook runs into it, that's the mill." I squinted forward into the early morning sun. Down, down the dizzying incline of the narrow gravel road which we were following, I could make out nothing except the sensation of falling over the edge into the deep, green gorge. I looked over my shoulder and caught a final glimpse of the sea as Nellie and Donald nonchalantly rumbled over the last crest, the lumber cart swinging behind us. From my seat the whole thing felt very precarious.

"Are you sure the horses can hold the wagon?" I finally got enough nerve to ask.

"I think we'll make it," smiled Grandfather. "Now if we were pulling a two-ton generator or something like that, I might be worried."

"Is that what runs the mill?"

"Yes."

"How did you get it down?"

"With horses—six of them. Hitched backwards."

"Backwards!"

"Horses can pull much more than they can hold, so I hitched them up so the generator went down first and it just pulled them down the hill, pulling them one step at a time."

"So they backed down?" I asked.

"Sort of. But because they were hitched backwards they could use their collars instead of the britching to hold the weight. There was quite a crowd out to see me lose my horses and the generator.

"But you didn't."

"No. The generator still runs the mill."

"Was Donald on that team?"

"No. It was before his time."

Donald and Nellie suddenly began to stroll perilously close to the edge of the cliff and my heart moved up another notch. But the team was just stopping for a drink at a roadside spring. They obviously knew the route and I told myself to relax. Would I be this nervous in a car? Probably not. But then in a car you didn't feel so exposed. There was all that metal between you and the edge of the road. From the cart you could smell the hot sun on the grass, feel the gentle breeze buffering against the trees. It was altogether different from being in a car.

In fact it was fine. Much better than peeping out a car window. Then a sudden, terrifying thought occurred.

"Grandpa!"

"Yes, Clive."

"What about rabbits?"

"They're lots of them."

"Oh, God! What will we do about Nellie? What if she spooks?"

"Don't worry. She can't drag Donald very far."

"He won't bolt?"

"Never has before and I think he's too old to change now."

"How come Donald's the quiet one? I would have thought it would have been the reverse." Grandpa shrugged.

"Donald was tame, even as a stallion. The children used to walk under his belly and he would never move. But Nellie is a different story. She was five or six when I bought her. I think she had been abused. In those days she would bolt at a butterfly. The man who sold her to me practically gave her away. He said he couldn't manage her."

"How did you train her?"

"Just a little patience. I used her with Donald as much as possible. She learned from him. One day I hitched her up alone and, sure enough, first chance, she grabbed the bit in her teeth and off she went. After a while she slowed down and I cracked the whip again. Well I made her run until her legs trembled—quite a session it was."

"What did that do?"

"Well, in those days, bolting for Nellie was a bit of a joke. She loved to do it. A butterfly or a bumblebee, and off she'd go like an express train. It was great fun. Worth the beating her former owner always gave her at the end of the run and so instead of beating her, I thought the trick was to take some of the fun out of the running."

"Did it work?"

"Pretty much. Unless something pops up right under her feet—like a rabbit—she keeps her peace."

Things certainly were peaceful. I looked back up the side of the mountains, now towering above us. We were only about three miles from home, but by the geography we could have been a hundred.

The road was beginning to level off into a manageable slope and the horses of their own accord broke into a fast trot. The lumber wagon swayed and jumped wildly. Grandfather shouted them down a bit and we rattled across the small wooden bridge at the end of the pond.

"There's the mill," said Grandfather.

What a disappointment it was. I had expected a large stone building with a waterwheel and a parking lot. Instead the mill was so humble it was difficult to make out if it was anything at all. A small shed covered what must have been the generator. The saw was exposed to the weather. A long, ramshackle carriage lay in front of the saw to carry the logs for cutting. There was plenty of sawdust around. Some logs and timber were stacked at odd angles and that was it. Some mill. Grandfather must have seen the disappointed look on my face.

"We don't use it much anymore, Clive. But in its time this little mill cut a good deal of wood. When your Dad was your age, we had five or six men working here every day, six days a week."

"Where is everyone now?"

Grandfather shrugged. "Who knows? I can barely keep track of my own family."

"Did my Dad ever operate the saw?" I looked at the wicked-looking teeth.

"No, the mill was always Gerard's responsibility. I guess you could say he was the boss."

"Roland's father."

"Yes."

"What's Uncle Gerard do now?"

"He owns a couple of trucks, hauls wood for the big mill in Margaree. There used to be five saw mills like this little one in Chéticamp alone. They're all closed. Here we used to cut all the finished timber, fence posts and slab for our parish. Everyone used to come. Seems strange now, doesn't it? Everything is so quiet."

"What made the mill close?"

"Times change, oil furnaces came in. I guess it's mostly because the young men aren't interested in farming any-more. Too little money. Better to work in the city . . . like your father."

Grandfather unhitched the horses and took them over to graze in the meadow while we began the business of loading the fence posts. I hadn't noticed the heat before but it seemed within a few seconds of lifting the posts my shirt was soaked with sweat. I took my shirt off. That was a mistake.

The gum from the bark on the posts stuck to my body instead of my shirt. With the help of the sticky-sweet sap and my own perspiration I began to resemble a delin-quent fir tree. But I sweated on, trying to copy Grandpa's style of lifting the posts from the pile to the truck with a swing and slight kick with his knee. It looked so easy. Still, there was a solid satisfaction in watching our load grow higher because new posts were needed, especially in the lane.

"Clive."

"Yes, Grandpa."

"Have you ever had spruce gum before?"

"No."

"See this stuff," he said, pointing with his pocket knife at an unappetizing lump of sap which had dried into a purplish clump on the bark. "That's spruce gum," and he cut off a piece with his pocket knife. "Try some, it's good."

"Why don't you try it first?" I asked.

"With my old teeth?" and Grandpa laughed. "I'd lose what few I have."

I didn't want to offend Grandpa, nor did I want to eat the gum. But there didn't seem to be any way out. "O.K., I'll try it." I bit into the unappetizing lump . . . it certainly was chewy. Very chewy. Very, very chewy. My teeth were going to come right out of their sockets. It sure didn't taste like anything I'd ever munched before.

We continued lifting the posts onto the timber truck, but the posts had become a secondary problem. I wondered if there was an Olympic event for chewing because I certainly was in heavy training for it. My jaw muscles ached with the effort but the flavour, once you got used to it, wasn't all that bad. A sweet, distinctive taste, but impossible to compare to anything else. Perhaps spruce gum was the reason Dad had such good teeth.

"Clive."

"Yes, Grandpa."

"I guess that'll do."

"But we're only three-quarters full."

"True enough, but the horses have to get it up the hill." I looked back up at the mountain. It was a good mile to the top. I had forgotten about that part. We had real horses, not mechanical ones. I didn't envy them.

We went down to the brook for a drink and I tried to rinse my shirt out. What a mess it was! Aunt Germaine was not going to be pleased.

"Don't worry about your shirt, Clive. We'll put it in a bucket of soapy water when we get home. That will take the gum off."

"But I can't eat lunch without a shirt!"

"When Germaine isn't looking, sneak through my bedroom and up the stairs and get a clean one."

"O.K. How come your shirt is clean, Grandpa?"

"It's a trick, that's all. You'll learn." I looked at Grandfather's large, muscular forearms as he washed his face and thought to myself it had something to do with strength also.

It was a long, heavy haul up the mountainside for the two horses. They leaned into their harness, straining mightily against the fierce tug of both gravity and the dead weight of the timber. The cart reluctantly followed. We walked, Grandpa driving from the side, stopping them every fifty yards or so for a breather. Then they were off again. Nellie, cagily, always a half-step behind big Donald so that he took more of the weight. Grandpa, in deference to her condition, let Nellie get away with it. It took us about forty-five minutes to reach the top; with a truck or a tractor it would have taken about ten minutes. As we ambled back down the farm lane, it struck me that when you got right down to it, it was the tractor that had killed Grandpa's mill. Just as the horse had replaced the oxen, so had the tractor supplanted the horse. Tractors and gasoline-powered trucks meant that you didn't need a saw mill every five or six miles. One every forty or fifty miles would do because you could drive forty miles in a truck about as fast as you could go five with a horse. At that moment the notion seemed to make perfect sense.

One of my first discoveries in Cape Breton was that we lived on earth. Before that I certainly knew we had earth. Earth was something you put things on or, conversely, it was something that had things on it. Generally you put pavement on top of earth—street pavement, school-ground pavement, sidewalk pavement, driveway pavement, parking lot pavement. Earth was black and dirty. There was lots of it.

The first intimations I had that we actually lived on earth occurred during the drive with my Uncle Phil from

Sydney Airport to the village—that unnerving sense of space as we drove towards the northern end of the island; of the earth curving under the sky. It's a sensation that can't be felt in the city. There's too much clutter, too many objects.

Earth isn't an easy feeling to get used to. At the beginning I was dogged by the feeling that Grandfather should have surrounded the house with trees and hedges; that there should be something to disguise the earth. It was unsettling. Earth should be like it is in the city, covered and placed delicately out of sight, to be glimpsed at occasionally while gardening. Yet, as the summer passed, I gradually outgrew my fear of living on earth. I'm not sure how it happened, only that it happened slowly. It had something to do with learning to expect distances in front of your eyes, to expect to be able to let your line of vision sweep along the coastline for miles and miles, or to look across fields up to the summer pastures and from there to the green mountains before your eyes met the blueness of the sky. It had something to do with lying in the grass on Sunday afternoon and swearing you could feel the earth slowly revolving beneath your back. It had something to do with hummocky pasture grass. It had something to do with the picked over barnyard and the green fields of timothy. Earth.

Grandpa rubbed the side of his cheek and regarded the little brown bull with a dubious eye while the little brown bull regarded him with equal suspicion.

"Well, what should we do? Should I drive him along with the rest of the cows back up to the high pasture? I'm not afraid," I said boldly, being certain from Grandpa's cavalier approach to the round-up the previous evening that there wasn't much to worry about.

"Well, I don't know. Usually I like to keep a bull with

the cows for the summer. It keeps them quiet and saves on artificial insemination."

"Oh," I said, uncomprehendingly.

"But I'm not sure about this fellow. He's a lot smaller than I thought he'd be. Almost all Hereford and little Ayrshire."

"Oh," I said again. He did seem to have shrunk in the barnyard.

"Hereford is a beef cow and Ayrshire is a dairy cow," continued Grandfather patiently. "A good cross gives you a hardy dual-purpose cow, good for both milk and the butcher. Works well around here, although the bigger farmers like them either dairy or beef."

"Well let's send him back up then," I said, anxious to try Donald at a pace faster than a walk. But Grandfather shook his head.

"No, no. He won't do. He's just too beefy. I should have been watching more closely."

"So what shall we do?"

"I'll get the government man in and we'll go with either dairy or beef," sighed Grandpa.

"What about the bull?"

"Keep him here for the moment."

"How?" I asked, seeing his close proximity to the old Ayrshire. He didn't look like he wanted to be separated.

"Easy," said Grandfather. "Bring the Ayrshire along, but catch her by the collar just before she goes through the gate."

Grandpa began to prod the young bull gently toward the corral in the night pasture. We got to the gate and I caught the Ayrshire by the collar. The bull ambled past through the gate and Grandpa closed it after him. Then Donald and I and the cows began the long morning shuffle up to the high pasture. The bull began bawling as we turned up the lane, but it was too late. He had been fooled. The old Ayrshire tried to double back but, using

horsemanship I didn't know I had, Donald and I kept
her plodding in front of us. With a great feeling of ac-
complishment we made it through the two sets of gates
and crossed the concession road without incident.

Once the cows were safely installed in the high pasture,
I was determined the trip home would be faster. So with
a firm "giddap," and a smart tap with my heels, I urged
my trusty steed forward. To my great surprise the huge
horse broke into a trot. It was terrifying. With each step
he took I seemed to bounce a little higher and come
down a little slower. The ground no longer looked soft
and hummocky. It looked hard and very far away. My
stirrups flew backwards and forwards. One foot came
out. "Whoa," I called out. Donald stopped immediately
and I was gracefully pitched headfirst over his shoulder
past his neck and down onto the ground with a bone-
crunching jar. I lay flat on my back, seeing a new version
of stars. Donald stuck his muzzle down on my chest en-
quiringly. He was a very understanding horse. I hadn't
been mistaken. The ground was hard. Everything
ached—my head, my neck, my back—yet everything
seemed to work. I should have been used to it by now.
Donald and I walked back to the barn. Grandpa was waiting for us.

"Clive!"

"Yes?"

"Beats me why you take the horse. You always come
back on foot."

"Good company," I replied, refusing to take the bait.

"Must be . . . What happened this time?"

"Donald started to trot and I just couldn't hang on."

"You fell off?"

"I fell off."

"Are you all right?"

"Sure."

"Watch this." Grandpa mounted Donald and began to

walk him around the barnyard. "You see, it's just like when you're driving from the buggy. The horse can't just wander along at his own pace. He's got to be listening to you." Ruefully I had to admit there was a difference to the horse's walk. His neck was arched, his ears cocked. Grandpa didn't even bother to give a voice command. A slight pressure from his heels and Donald began to trot. "Are you watching, Clive?"

"Yes, I am, Grandpa."

"See. I'm not letting the horse throw me up. I'm using my knees and stirrups to push up and then come down. Trotting is difficult. It's a short, choppy motion and you've got to work at staying in time with the up-and-down motion. If you get out of sequence and start your bum coming down when the horse's back is coming up, there's only one place you're going."

"On the ground."

"Right. He's bigger than you are." Grandpa pulled up Donald next to me and dismounted, his breath coming a bit short. "Want to try it?"

"Sure." I climbed up, my knees shaking slightly.

"Don't start right away. Give the horse a chance. Watch your hands. Not so hard on his mouth. That's it. O.K. Anytime you're ready." I sucked in my breath and said in an almost inaudible voice, "Giddap." Donald began to trot. I stood up in the stirrups and as I was coming down I felt Donald's broad, powerful back coming to greet me and I went sailing dangerously upwards, my heels already beginning to lose contact with the stirrups. "Rein him in, Clive! Rein him in."

"Whoa." Donald slowed abruptly to a walk, but this time I stayed on.

"Try again, Clive, but remember you've got to start with him. You were just a second or so late that time." I nodded but I was beginning to feel desperate. I didn't even know what Grandpa meant by starting with him. We were still *ensemble*—what more could there be?

"How will I know that I'm doing it right?"

"Because you won't go flying. You'll feel the rhythm. Now off you go," and Donald, listening to Grandpa's voice rather than mine, began to trot once more. But this time by some lucky coincidence, I was in tune with Donald's stride. When my bum came back down to the saddle it didn't get cracked back up to the sky. Remembering Grandpa's advice, I pushed up from the stirrups to go with the horse, came back down gently and for a few more magical moments, horse and rider were in harmonious company before I lost the rhythm on a turn and began to flail dangerously around in the air once more. Donald stopped of his own accord. Apparently he didn't like his back being pummelled any more than I did. I slid out of the saddle a bit shakily but triumphant.

"I can do it, Grandpa!"

"So you can, Clive. So you can. A little more practice and you'll be galloping home."

"Can you show me how to gallop?" I asked, but Grandfather laughed.

"Another time."

"But what's it like to gallop?"

"A gallop is like a rocking chair. You just sit. Nothing to it. Now let's go. We've got other things to do."

"Like what?"

"Call the vet for one."

"Is Nellie O.K.?"

"She's fine. It's the heifer."

"The yellow-brown cow?"

"Yes," said Grandfather briefly and turned to walk towards the house before I could pester him with more questions. I had seen her yesterday. She had looked all right, quietly resting in the summer box-stall. I unsaddled Donald and tethered him in the stall. Before I left I poured a small cannister of oats into his feed bowl. It was strictly illegal. Grandpa didn't like to see the horses getting more than one feed a day. Oats. Small hard grains.

They didn't look very exciting to me but old Donald would have sold his horseshoes for a mouthful. He nickered with pleasure as they spilled from the metal scoop into his tray. I was just putting the scoop back into the oat bin when a strange, strangled groan echoed through the barn. I froze. It was a completely foreign sound. I had never heard anything like it before. I couldn't make out whether the cry had been human or animal, whether it had come from heaven or earth or somewhere in between. Then it came again, the same low, resonant groan. But this time there was no mistaking the origin of the cry. It was coming from the summer box-stall.

I hurried down the corridor, past the empty stalls and up the ladder towards the outside box-stall. As I entered, another low painful groan greeted me. The yellow cow was no longer resting comfortably. She was stretched out in the straw, her eyes half shut, her mouth frothing. With each groan her whole body convulsed with terrible force. Then I noticed a tiny foot showing from her hind end. The cow convulsed again but the little foot disappeared. I ran up to the house as fast as my legs could carry me, crying, "Grandpa! Grandpa!" long before he had any chance of hearing me. When I entered the kitchen Grandpa was quietly pouring some tea for himself and Aunt Germaine.

"Grandpa, did you call the vet?"

"Yes, he'll be here in an hour or so."

"Have some tea and cookies," said Aunt Germaine.

"Grandpa, I saw the cow." I stopped my description there, uncertain exactly how to continue a rather delicate subject in front of Aunt Germaine.

"Well?" said Grandpa rather impatiently.

"A foot was sticking out," I said rather lamely. There was a moment of utter silence. Then Grandpa put his tea cup down and went over to begin lacing his boots. Aunt Germaine filled a bucket with hot, soapy water. Grandfather picked up the bucket and I followed.

Nothing had changed with the cow. She lay still, but she would groan and her belly would twist. "Are you sure you saw a hoof, Clive?"

"Yes, I swear I did."

"Well, it shouldn't be too hard then." And Grandpa began to scrub his hands and forearms in the soapy water. Then he lay down beside the cow and began to search for the foot. It didn't take long. "I've got one, but the other is folded forward. That's why she can't push him out."

"Can you bring it back?"

"I don't know. I might break it. Here, pass me that heavy twine. We'll get this one leg secure anyway." The cow heaved once more. She relaxed and Grandpa stretched out and tried to work the little leg around. But after what seemed an age he finally gave up. "God, it's frustrating," muttered Grandfather between breaths. "She's that close," indicating with a finger, "to bringing him out."

"I guess we'll have to wait for the vet," I said. Grandfather nodded wearily.

"If she makes it that long. Let's give it one more try. When she pushes, you pull on the good leg—not hard, just a good steady pull—and I'll try and pop the bent leg through." The cow began to heave. I pulled gently on the leg, afraid I would break it. "Harder," cried Grandfather. Then suddenly as if by magic the other tiny hoof popped out in Grandpa's hand. "O.K. Perfect. Now on the next contraction, pull." We pulled and the little calf's bottom appeared. Then the body, and finally the head, and suddenly a brand-new, white and brown calf was standing before us. It was magic. A profound and wonderful magic. The cow raised her head weakly but seemed unable to rise. "Let's give her a hand, Clive." Grandpa picked the calf up and brought it over to her head where she could see him. But she still made no effort to rise.

"She's a mess," I said, trying to keep my voice matter of

fact, but my heart was hammering at express train speed.

"That she is."

"What are we going to do?"

"Well, first we'll get this wee one educated," and Grandpa directed the stumbling steps of the calf to his mother's udder where, to my amazement, he began to nurse almost immediately. "Secondly we clean up. The afterbirth goes in the manure shed. Bury it." I must have looked a little green because Grandpa said, "I'll do it. You throw down some fresh straw." By the time we had the stall cleaned up, the yellow cow was showing a bit more interest in her surroundings but she was still stretched out.

"Is there anything we can do now?" I asked.

"Best wait for the vet," said Grandpa quietly.

"Speak of the devil," said a large man as he stepped through the doorway. He was carrying a square black case.

"Jean," said Grandfather with relief flooding into his voice. "It's good to see you." The vet came over and bent down beside the calf.

"This guy seems to be in fine shape. A little on the small side but he'll grow." Then he looked up at Grandfather.

"What's wrong with the cow?"

"Won't stand up."

"Anything else?"

"Not that I can tell," said Grandfather shrugging.

"A few stitches in her bum and a shot of adrenalin should fix her up," said the vet calmly as he opened his black case. Just then the cow's whole body shuddered with a giant contraction. The silence which followed the poor cow's groan was profound. Only a slight breeze against the shingles reminded me of life. It was as if for a few split seconds we were all posing for some hidden photographer, the doctor kneeling by his black case, Grandfather standing with his hand against the door frame, me squatting by the cow's head.

"Well," said Grandfather finally. "Well, well, well." Grandfather always said "well, well, well" in the most unfathomable of circumstances.

"What's your name, lad?" asked the vet.

"Clive. Clive Doucet."

"A Fernand, William?"

"C'est ça."

"Clive, can you go to the house and get another bucket of warm, soapy water?"

"Yes, sir." And off I went. At the house Aunt Germaine wanted to know how things were going.

I said, "Fine," and hurried back with the bucket of water. The vet washed up like Grandfather had done, right up to the shoulder, and then proceeded to examine the cow.

"Damnation," said the vet, a slow smile lighting his face. "Doesn't that beat all. She's got twins."

"Is it alive?" asked Grandfather.

"You bet it is," said the vet. "If I can just get him turned, I'll have him out in a minute. There, that's it." The cow's belly contracted once more and another tiny pair of hooves appeared. Then once again a tiny rear end, body and head. He didn't look very good. Unlike the first, he couldn't stand.

"Pass me some of that clean straw, quick!" I did so. And the vet began to rub him vigorously with the straw. Slowly the calf started to perk up, his skin colour changing gradually from bluish to pink. "Clive, you keep rubbing him. William, pass me my bag." The little calf kicked feebly with one back leg. He was alive, but just. The vet cleaned his mouth and eyes with a moist sponge. The little fellow stirred, stood for a second and then gently collapsed by his mother's udder. We quickly placed the tiny calf closer to its mother but the calf did not stir. His breathing seemed to become even more ragged. "If he won't eat, we'll do it for him," and the vet and Grandfather began squirting milk down the calf's throat. "Hold the other one back," ordered the vet, and I grabbed the first calf, holding him tight to my chest. The vet continued and the warm milk seemed to inject life into the calf. Soon he was sucking noisily and his brother was straining in my arms to join him. Just then the cow tried to rise, her hind hoof coming within an inch of breaking the vet's arm and crushing the calf.

"Damn fool," said Grandfather, and sat on her neck. The cow grunted and lay back down. "Everything O.K. back there?" called Grandfather.

"Everything's fine," said the vet. "You've got twins, William. Two healthy steers for the price of one. Isn't that something."

"Guess that artificial insemination can't be all bad," said Grandpa with a grin.

"Is it unusual?" I asked a bit surprised. Twins didn't seem to be such a big deal.

"Oh, about once every hundred thousand births," said the vet. "I bet your Grandad never saw twin births before, or have you, William?"

"Not alive."

"Nor have I," said the vet proudly. "It's a first. Mind if I bring old Doc McDougall round tomorrow? He'd like to see them."

"Sure," said Grandfather expansively.

"Might as well let her up now, William," said the vet.

"O.K.," said Grandfather and he freed the cow's neck. She looked around at him as if mistrusting his intentions, then with much grunting rolled over on her knees and then stood. I let go of the calf I was holding and he wasted no time moving toward the dinner table.

"Well, that's that," said the vet, as if reluctant to admit that really was that.

"Any special instructions?" asked Grandfather.

"Yes, there is, come to think of it. Watch that she doesn't reject one of them."

"Keeps one from feeding?"

"That's it. Nothing spectacular."

"Can I stay then?" I asked.

"Good idea," said Grandpa. "I'm beat. Cup of tea, Jean?" The vet smiled and nodded. They left, leaving me alone with two calves and one nervous mother cow, or perhaps confused was a better word. She would sniff one calf and begin licking it. Then the other would shove in her line of vision and she'd leave the first to sniff the second curiously, then with interest. Then she'd start licking it until the first attracted her attention and the exercise would begin all over again. It was as if she couldn't quite understand why there were two, but eventually in a stumbling sort of way she got them both cleaned. The calves suckled briefly and then as if on a mutual signal they folded up side by side in a pile of deep hay close to the manger. The cow continued to lick them, apparently trying to reassure herself that everything was as it should be. Then she made a soft sound in her throat. She too lay down but this time she did it carefully so that her huge body settled close by the young ones, yet her hooves remained safely out of their way.

I stood up, my legs cramped from squatting. They trembled slightly. This birthing business was quite exhausting.

Alfred

What was that irritating noise? I struggled to rise from
morning sleep and could not. Why should I anyway? The
bed was a perfect place to be, comfortably cradling my
body on cloudy wings of sleep. I turned away from the
window, descending lazily several thousand feet to rest
on a mossy shelf. But the irritating noise at the window
continued. Ping . . . ping . . . ping. What was it anyway? A
bird? I rolled off my mossy shelf and floated gently to the
ground, where I remembered it was Sunday morning
and the pinging noise was probably my cousin Roland. I
went to the window still somewhat groggy and signalled
to him that I was awake, dressed as quietly as I could and
tip-toed downstairs. It was 5:30 and still quite dark. No
breakfast today. I went straight outside and joined
Roland. He was carrying a small rifle.

"Where did you get that?" I asked.

"From Joe. He lent it to me."

"Does your father know?"

"Sort of."

"Does he know or doesn't he?"

"I kind of told him."

"What do you mean, 'Kind of'?"

"I said we would probably borrow Joe's 22."

"What did he say?"

"He said, 'Don't.' "

"That's what I thought," I said. "My dad wouldn't let
me have a rifle either. You'd better leave it here."

"No," said Roland stubbornly. "I'm taking it."

"Why? We're trapping rabbits, not shooting them."

"What if Grandfather finds it?" said Roland.

"He won't tell your father."

"Yes, he will," said Roland positively and on reflection I had to agree. "Let's go," said Roland, perceiving he had the advantage and resolutely set off for the summer pasture. I waffled for a few more seconds, uncertain about what to do and then followed him. We walked along in silence for some time. The only sound was the wet grass slapping against our boots. I shivered partly from excitement and partly from the chill. I looked at my watch— 5:45. Grandpa wouldn't be getting up for another fifteen minutes or so. I couldn't quite believe the snares we had so carefully set last night could possibly trap anything. Surely the rabbits wouldn't be so stupid as to run wide-eyed right into the looped wire? But Roland had assured me they were. They just hopped down their little bunny trail, nose to the ground, just like they did every morning, entered the loop of wire with their heads, but were unable to make it through. Apparently they didn't have the sense to be still and quietly retire. They thrashed around violently, pulling the wire tighter and tighter until they died.

"Clive."

"Yes."

"Quiet."

"I'm not saying anything."

"Look over there." I looked up in the direction Roland was pointing and finally saw what he was making the fuss about. It was a deer—a large, antlered animal. He was standing only about a hundred yards away from us, head down, chewing grass lazily like a cow.

"What's it doing down here?" I asked, a bit shocked that a wild animal should be so close to the house.

"Sometimes they come down from the mountains in the summer to graze."

"He doesn't seem afraid of us."

"Hasn't seen us yet and the wind is blowing from him to us, so he hasn't picked up our smell."

"Are you going to shoot him?" I asked curiously.

"Are you crazy, Clive! Hunting season doesn't open until October."

"Oh, I didn't know. It just seemed like such a good opportunity," I whispered.

"It is," said Roland in a somewhat mournful tone. The deer's head came up from his grazing and suddenly he was staring at us directly. In the next instant he was striding towards the mountains. In a few seconds he had vanished over the far hill. We plodded on alone.

We climbed the last hill before entering the woods which plunged down to the edge of the pond.

"Roland?"

"Yes?"

"Do you think we'll get any?"

"Last fall I got nine in one morning."

"Nine! That's amazing. What did you do with them all?"

"Ate them."

"All nine?"

"Sure. Mom made some pies and froze them. Rabbits aren't that big. It takes about three rabbits for one pie— sometimes four, depending on the size."

"What do they taste like?"

"Delicious," said Roland with fervour. "You haven't tasted anything until you've tasted rabbit pie."

"That's what Grandpa said about lobster."

"Did you like it?"

"Yes," I replied, remembering the merry evening when Grandpa, Germaine and I had demolished eight lobsters between us. With the huge pot steaming on the stove and the bowls of hot butter, eating lobster had been more of a festival than a meal. If rabbits tasted anything like lobster, they were certainly worth catching. Catching? You don't catch rabbits—you snare them, I told myself scornfully, while at the back of my mind hovered the baleful word, "KILL." We entered the woods and began following one or two of the narrow paths down to the Salt Pond that served the rabbits as a highway. I followed Roland as quietly as possible, directing my feet into the soft prints his own feet made. Nevertheless we seemed to add a great deal of noise to the early morning stillness. We came around the first sharp curve in the path to our first snare. There was nothing in it. I didn't quite know whether to be relieved or disappointed but there was no mistaking Roland's feelings.

"Damn. If we can't get one here, there's not much hope further on."

"Why's that?"

"This loop is perfectly situated. The path is steep, the rabbit comes around the curve and bang—it's all over."

"Let's try further on," I said.

"Haven't got much choice, have we?" said Roland as he pocketed the wire. But it was the same story all the way down to the lake—all our carefully placed wires were empty. Roland's jacket pocket bulged with the wire he had retrieved from the path. "I should have known better," grumbled Roland.

"Why's that?"

"*Les lièvres courent pas en août.* It's an old expression and it's true."

"But we're not in August," I replied. "It's only June."

"Doesn't matter. It's too hot. Look at us. We're sweating and we just walked down the mountain. The rabbits just browse in this weather. They don't run. In October, every one of those snares would have had a fat rabbit in it."

"Well, thanks for bringing me along anyway, Roland. I really enjoyed it," I said looking across the still water of the pond.

"You did?"

"Sure. I won't be around in October, remember?"

"Oh yes, that's right. Well, we might as well start the climb back up. Somehow it always seems easier if you're carrying a few rabbits for the pot."

"Want me to carry the gun back up?"

"No, it's O.K.," said Roland, and we began the long climb back up from the pond to the summer pasture.

We walked steadily, leaning into the steep slant of the mountainside. This time we paid no attention to the noise of our passage, only to the pull of gravity. I half expected to stumble upon a veritable flock of rabbits all up and about now that the snares were down but we saw nothing, which wasn't surprising as my eyes were mostly focused on the footing in the first few feet of trail in front of me. We climbed and I began to understand how a rabbit could quite easily go hopping straight into one of Roland's cleverly placed snares. One minute they would be pursuing their regular path, the next struggling in the looped wire.

When we finally emerged from the shade of the woods into the summer pasture, my sides were heaving and my shirt sticky, but Roland didn't stop. He pushed on up the now grassy hill.

"Hey, Roland! Can't we take a break?" I called, sitting down on a log at the edge of the woods. Suddenly a large animal jumped out from almost under my feet. I yelled with surprise and fright. When I shouted, Roland turned to face me and saw it at almost the same instant I did. He knelt and fired a quick shot. The animal tumbled forward and began to writhe in the grass. Roland hurried over to the animal and from the distance of just a few feet, shot again.

"Come on over, Clive. It's O.K. He's dead."

"What is it?" I asked, noticing my voice was several octaves higher than it usually was.

"A hare. Big one too." I advanced cautiously across the fifteen yards or so that separated me from the animal. It was brown. On one side of the rabbit's body were two neat round holes, on the other a thick, red spaghetti of blood and guts. The animal's back legs convulsed spasmodically, pushing its nose into the grass, eyes bulging and glassy. It didn't look dead to me.

"Nice shot," I said casually, then walked back to the log and threw up, or tried to, but there was nothing in my stomach.

"Lucky we didn't snare any bunnies," said Roland in good humour.

"Isn't that a rabbit?"

"It's a hare."

"What's the difference?" I asked, regaining control of my heaving sides.

"Hares are bigger, about three or four times the size of a rabbit. This fellow must weigh about ten pounds. A rabbit is only good for two or three."

"Where did you learn to shoot so well?"

"Mostly out here with Joe. You ready to go now."

"Yes, I'm fine. Sorry."

"Nothing to be sorry about, cuz," said Roland tranquilly. "I didn't feel so great the first time either."

Cuz? Short for cousin. I had never been called that before. It felt just right . . . cuz. I stood up and hitched my trousers up. "What are we going to do with it?" I asked.

"Cook it. What else?

"Can we take it home?" I asked, doubtfully, thinking of Uncle Gerard's last words on the rifle. Roland looked down at the hare, the bright, glassy terror turned opaque, the wet guts already drying in the sun.

"We'll have to butcher it first. Dad won't know how we killed it then."

"Do you know how?" I asked unnerved once more.

"Of course! Who do you think skins the rabbits—my mother? She'd pass out first. We'll do it at Joe's. I've got to return the rifle anyway."

"O.K.," I replied. Roland casually picked the hare up

by the heels and we set off across the field for the Chiasson's.

Three great piles of wood dominated the crest of the hill between the house and the barn. The largest was composed of hardwood blocks for the furnace; then there were soft wood slats for kindling; and the third pile was a finer, mixed cut for the kitchen stove. Sheltered between these wooden hills were a couple of well-used chopping blocks and one rather rickety saw horse. The open side of the wood yard faced towards the sea and provided a magnificent view while the piled wood protected the wood cutter from any unkindly breezes. It was a grand place to loaf, which looking back strikes me as curious because splitting wood is usually depicted as the hallmark of the hard-working small farmer. In actual fact, it was an in-between kind of chore—something you did when there was nothing much else pressing. And there was nothing more in-between than filling in time just before supper. It was a good deal like reading the evening newspaper—a time for gossip and speculation on the state of the world. The day's work was pretty well done. Dinner was just around the corner. Consequently, splitting stove wood required a good deal of leaning, pausing and good conversation. Like all the farm chores I was learning, splitting wood looked easy and was actually damn difficult. A razor-sharp axe and a heavy block of wood can quickly combine to frustrate and injure the apprentice axeman, although to have watched Grandfather you wouldn't have believed it. He would casually split the largest of blocks with one or two easy strokes.

"There's a trick to it, Clive," Grandpa would say with a conspiratorial grin. I would sigh, put my axe down and receive my ninety-third lecture on the care and handling of an axe. Basically the trick came down to this: first you had to have an eye for the lie of the grain in the wood. The grain told you where the block of wood was likely to break most easily. Secondly you must have the ability to hit that exact spot dead on more than once. Then came the hard part. As your blade struck the wood, you had to turn the blade just a fraction in order that the block was stressed both vertically and horizontally—simultaneously—although Grandfather didn't quite explain it that way.

"Damn it, Clive. You're going to cut your foot off! Let the heel of the blade strike first. Watch me. See if the heel strikes first. If your aim isn't quite true, the axe will bounce away, not towards you." I tried again. "That's it. You have to keep your left hand lower than your right. . . . Is something bothering you? You don't seem to be your old self."

"No, I'm O.K."

"You're mad about something? . . . Is it because Germaine yelled at you for forgetting to take your boots off?"

"I guess. She always seems to be angry at me or something. I don't think she likes me very much."

"She likes you fine. That's just the way Germaine is. Here, put the axe down for a moment. You can't chop your way through to China. I've tried often enough." I put my axe down. The truth was I was feeling blue. Lately Germaine always seemed to in bad humour and I often seemed to be the cause. I glumly watched the late evening sun splash a fiery red paint across the sea, a sight I normally found quite wonderful. "Don't worry so much, Clive," said Grandfather. "I've never seen such a worrier—unless it was your grandmother," and he laughed. "It's not your fault Germaine yelled at you. She just can't help it. Germaine is highly strung, that's all."

"But I did forget to take my boots off," I said.

"If you'd remembered to take your boots off, it would have been something else. That's just the way she is."

"She must have scared all her boyfriends away," I grumbled.

"Perhaps," said Grandfather slowly. "It's my guess she never really wanted to be married. As a young girl I can remember she would spend days in her room crying. We sent her to the best doctors in Halifax, but nothing seemed to work. In the end she gave up school which she was very good at. I've even heard your father say she was the brightest one of the lot, yet she never went past grade eight or nine. And when she was older, Germaine did chase her boyfriends away. She seemed to want to stay home. Often she was very sad. Your grandmother and I never understood Germaine. She was always different from the rest. There's nothing you can do." Grandfather went back to chopping wood and then he stopped. "We'll have to have a birthday party next week."

"Who for?"

"Germaine. She'll be forty."

The birthday party had started quietly enough. Aunt Germaine had liked her presents. Bernadette had sent a new dress. There was a new scarf, new shoes. Madame Cormier had baked a giant three-tier cake. Then David Boudreau had arrived with his fiddle and a huge box of beer.

The music of the fiddle still sang in my head. For such a big man, David could certainly move around, his fingers dancing up and down the tiny instrument, the bow flying back and forth while his whole body urged the fiddle on as he stepped and swayed in time with the music. I couldn't quite figure out if Germaine's party was a success or not. Grown-ups behaved in a rather strange way at parties. Such a lot of shouting and carrying on—it seemed rather nervous-making to me. I had never seen my aunt drink before. It was quite a shock. The beer, in fact, was the reason *I* was standing in cold water up to my knees at the bottom of the well.

The well water was not just cold—it was ice cold. A small piece of sky glittered above. I could hear nothing. No music, no night sounds. Surely someone would come soon? I didn't want to try climbing out again. On the other hand, shivering to death wasn't a great idea either. Coming down had been so easy. I had just taken the rope in my hands and, using my feet to keep me off the wall, slid down. Once I was at the bottom, though, the plan had come unstuck. I couldn't reach the milk can without getting in the water, which I had done. But the water had been slightly deeper than I had anticipated and had begun to leak over the top of my rubber boots. Ignoring the water, I retied the milk can to the rope and then proceeded to climb back out, but it wasn't so easy. My boots kept slipping against the smooth, wet walls, throwing my weight entirely on my arms. Shinnying up the rope was impossible because it lay flat against the wall of the well. I had to be able to push away from it. So I sat on top of the milk can and waited. Soon the last beer in the frig would be exhausted and someone would come looking for the reserve supply which was chilling safely in the milk can.

I couldn't get over how cold it was. On the surface it had been a humid, summer night. In the well it was like an ice box. The small muscles along the sides of my ribs were shivering independently as if they were counting my ribs and forever arriving at the wrong total. Why hadn't I got a ladder, I asked myself for the umteenth time. Then my teeth began to chatter. At first it was kind of amusing until I realized I couldn't control the sound. Better try to climb out again. I grasped the rope firmly and pushed off with my feet. One step, two steps—and then my legs slipped down the wall leaving me smashed up against the side of the well. I lowered myself into the icy water once more, my arms shaking, my legs already feeling numb from the cold.

Damn it. This was ridiculous! Why didn't someone come? I banged at the milk can in pure frustration. The lid flew off and clanged against the stone wall. Nothing inside but the beer Grandfather and I had placed there in the afternoon to chill for the party. It certainly was cold now. Wait a minute. Beer had alcohol inside it. Wasn't alcohol supposed to keep you warm? A picture of a trusty St. Bernard flashed across my mind, a small barrel tied to his collar. I took one of the bottles out. No bottle opener here. But there was a way of taking the cap off. I had seen David Boudreau do it. You put the steel cap against the edge of a hard surface—a rough stone would do—then you leaned on the side of the cap with the heel of your hand . . . nothing happened. I leaned harder. The serrated edge of the cap was biting into the stone nicely but still nothing. Then a soft, hissing sound greeted my efforts. I pressed harder and with a sigh the cap bent in half and came off. Success. Shivering violently, I took a deep draught of the beer. It was freezing cold and it tasted horrible . . . like dirty shoes.

How did Grandpa drink this stuff? Cautiously, I took another sip . . . bubbly old shoes. No wonder grown-ups wanted it cold—to kill the taste. Didn't make you warmer, either. Perhaps I hadn't drunk enough. But what was considered enough? A half bottle? A whole bottle? I remembered David Boudreau had cases of the stuff stacked in his wood shed. I finished the bottle determinedly and opened another. I wondered if the Lone Ranger drank beer? Hardly likely. He was a clean-living guy. Clean-living guys never drank beer. But Grandpa drank beer and he was clean living—only on special occasions though, like birthdays. Perhaps birthdays made it right. Maybe the Lone Ranger drank beer on birthdays—his horse's birthday. He was very attached to his horse whom he called "Big Fellow." I took another swig. The brown liquid didn't taste quite so bad as it had before. I began tearing the beer label off. Confirmed beer drinkers always did this. They would take a sip and then tear a small strip off the label. Take a sip and tear another small strip off the label until the label sat in a little mound by the bottle. I supposed the beer companies gave you more money for the returned bottles if they were clean of labels. But I had better stop tearing the label apart here. The well water didn't need paper floating around in it. I took another swig. Beats ginger ale, that's for sure.

Another bottle, *monsieur*? I haven't finished this one, *garçon*. Better serve that frog over there, though—he looks thirsty. But frogs don't drink beer, *monsieur*. Serve him a little wine then. Everyone drinks wine. It's very refined. "Mr. Frog, would you like a little wine?" The little, green frog regarded me with his glassy, multi-faceted eyes and then said,

"Young man, you are getting drunk."

"That's interesting," I replied, looking into his emerald eyes. "How do you know?"

"Normally people don't talk to frogs when they're sober," said the frog.

"That's true," I replied reasonably, "but normally you don't find people sitting on a milk can at the bottom of a well, either. Or maybe this is all a dream. Maybe I'm safe asleep in my bed."

"Impossible," said the little green frog. "I am not imaginary, no matter what you may think."

"Oh . . . How do you stand the cold?" I asked the frog, anxious to either wake up or get warm.

"I do not like the cold," the frog snapped somewhat irritably. "This dank hole is perfectly ghastly. I shall be glad to be rid of it."

"Then what are you doing here?"

"I fell in, just like you did—in fact, when you did. One

moment I was jumping out of the way of your great clod-hoppers and the next thing I knew, I was falling down into this horrible habitat."

"Horrible habitat . . ." I acknowledged. "That's quite a mouthful."

"For a frog, you were going to say," said the frog in a tone that had slipped from irritable to angry.

"No, no. Not at all. I was just surprised, that's all."

"Oh," said the frog somewhat mollified. A silence descended on our conversation. I wasn't inclined to start talking again. He could get along by himself. I would imagine I was talking to someone else. I would not talk to the frog. I took another swig of the beer and paddled my feet in the water. Horrible habitat. I hadn't thought of it in exactly those words but they certainly summed the situation up—dank, cold and dark. I craned my neck back to catch another view of the patch of night sky. It seemed to have become smaller. I could hear the little frog shuffle around on his rocky perch. He cleared his throat.

"My name is Alfred," said the frog.

"Oh," I said, not particularly wanting to encourage the conversation.

"You may call me Alfred if you wish."

"Thank you," I said.

"I was wondering—do you mind if I talk to you?" asked Alfred a trifle nervously.

"Not at all," I replied, intrigued at his sudden sensitivity, but I kept my head resolutely directed at the dripping, rocky wall in front of me. Alfred cleared his throat once again.

"Well I was wondering . . . er . . . how do you expect to get us out of this predicament?"

"Us?"

"That is correct—us," said Alfred precisely. "It's your fault I'm down here."

"Yes, I had forgotten that," I said and took another sip of the beer. An acquired taste—that's what Dad said about beer. I burped. The sound echoed for the longest time around the stone walls. "Excuse me," I said, my apology out of keeping with the length and strength of the burp.

"Well, I'm waiting," said Alfred, ignoring my rumbling stomach.

"For what?"

"Your answer."

"What answer?"

"How are we going to get out of here?"

"Oh, it's quite simple. Grandfather should notice I'm missing soon. He'll come looking for me, or David Boudreau will come looking for the beer. Either way they'll find us, lower a ladder down—the big one with the extension—and out I'll climb."

"That may be fine for you," said Alfred crossly, "but it doesn't help me. I can't climb a ladder." I thought about this for a moment. There was no mistaking it. Alfred did have a problem.

"There's a simple solution," I said finally.

"What?"

"I'll carry you out."

"I don't trust you," said Alfred.

"Why not?"

"Because you're drunk."

"I am not drunk," I said mildly.

"Well, you might drop me."

"Not if you're in my shirt pocket."

"That sounds safe," said Alfred.

"Well come on over," I said.

"If you don't mind I'll wait until they lower the ladder."

"Suits me," I said equably, taking another swig of beer.

"I wish they'd hurry up, though," said Alfred. "I like it less and less down here."

"I'm not keen on the place either. Maybe I'll try and

climb out again." But to my surprise my arms seemed to have turned to lead. I sat back down on the milk can with a thump.

"Looks like we're here for a while yet," said Alfred dryly.

"Don't be a prig," I muttered.

"What's a prig?"

"S-s-someone who comments on the obvious unintelligently."

"You're not as dumb as you look," said Alfred, a touch of admiration slipping into his voice at my quick reply. As for myself, I was astounded, both at my own glibness and the definite slur at the start of 'someone.' Maybe Alfred was right, maybe I was getting drunk. I'd better not drink any more. Finish this one and call it a day, as Mr. Boudreau would say. Might be interesting to try another sentence and see if the slur reappeared. I composed a sentence carefully in my head before attempting it. "Wha . . . dyou . . . do . . . foraliving, Alfred?"

"Pardon?" said Alfred politely.

"Eschuse me," I said carefully. There had been no mistaking it—this time I had mangled several words badly. Better try again. "What . . . do . . . you . . . do . . . for . . . a . . . living?"

"I'm a dancer," said Alfred, again very politely. "In fact, I was just going to rehearsal when I . . . er . . . came across you, or vice versa, if you see what I mean?"

"Yes, I do," I said, gravely concentrating. "A dancer."

"What about you?" asked Alfred. "What do you do for a living?" Was it my imagination, or was Alfred being irritatingly polite?

"I . . . haven't . . . decided . . . yet. I'm . . . only . . . a . . . young . . . frog, I . . . mean . . . person."

"You're very big for a young person," said Alfred doubtfully. I nodded in sober agreement.

"Don't you think we should sing?" I asked.

"Why?" replied Alfred.

"Well, we can't dance," I said looking around and, without further debate, began to sing:

> *There's a hole in my bucket, dear Liza, dear Liza.*
> *There's a hole in my bucket, dear Liza, today.*
> *Then fix it, dear Henry, dear Henry, dear Henry.*
> *Then fix it, dear Henry, dear Henry, fix it.*
> *With what shall I fix it, dear Liza, dear Liza?*
> *With what shall I fix it, dear Liza, today?*

I can clearly remember singing those verses and many, many more. My voice echoed joyfully, noisily around the walls, but after that my memory becomes spotty. I can't remember climbing out of the well, but I can remember David Boudreau's voice roaring up at Germaine. "The boy's as drunk as a lord!" and Aunt Germaine shrieking in reply, "My God, what will we tell Fernand?" And I can remember Alfred jumping out of my shirt pocket onto Germaine's clean kitchen floor and me crawling after him calling, "Alfred! Alfred! You can't dance here." And I can remember, before falling asleep, the chatter of voices and music outside my bedroom door that advanced and receded like some nightmare tide. I was dying—that much was clear.

Jobs

I don't think that I had ever seen the sky until I came to Cape Breton Island. In the city, even a smallish city like Ottawa, there's always something between you and the sun, hence my myopic city senses had very little appreciation for the sky. Is it raining? Is it sunny? That was my rough sense of the heavens. The night sky didn't exist. It was just a blackness above the streetlights—a nothing—and the day sky, a patch of blue or grey glimpsed between buildings.

It took me a long time to figure out that the sunset belongs to the sky, not to the edge of the earth and from there that the sky begins in a feeling—a feeling that comes from living under it—of seeing each night the immense, marvellous diamond oceans which encircle all travellers on this little planet. Feeling the first timid rays of our sun warm the morning meadows until the mist is gone and there is only a careening, jig-saw sky of endless colours that fade and grow and change in a giant bowling game of blues and greys which continue ricocheting long after the bald sun prints its flashing, inky red goodbye. Of the twilight that hangs between our two dimensions. The sky, our third and most wondrous dimension.

"Grandpa, what did you like doing best before you started farming?" Grandpa finished splitting the block he was working on before he replied.

"You mean which job?"

"Yes."

"I liked them all. No, that's not true. I didn't much like being a miner in Inverness. That was the only job I ever quit."

"What happened?"

"Nothing much. I had been working there for about six months down in the mine and I got a cold. Nothing much. I just didn't feel quite right so I came up about noon. It was winter. The sun was sparkling off the snow—little crystals of light everywhere I looked. I handed in my gear and never went back again."

"Where did you go after that?"

"Back to the farm, then onto another job. I was only nineteen or so at the time. Michel Poirier and I had this plan to save a thousand dollars each and then go out west. We figured everyone was a millionaire on the prairies."

"Did you go?"

"Does it look like it?" laughed Grandpa. "But Michel did. He bought himself a whole section."

"How come you never went, Grandpa?"

"My father died just before we were supposed to leave. I was the eldest in the family so I had to stay and help out." Grandpa went back to chopping wood, his arms moving in easy, rhythmical strokes. No talking. That was what Grandpa's work said to me. No talking. But I couldn't help it. The question popped out. "What happened to Michel? Did he ever come back?"

"Just once, a long time later. I had a family of my own then. And so did he out in Alberta."

"Had he done well?"

"Yes, he loved it. Had pictures of the farm. It looked fine."

"Grandpa?"

"Yes, Clive."

"Stop for a moment. You still haven't told me about your favourite job." Grandpa looked at me, a bit exasperated, but sunk his axe into the chopping block anyway.

"Let's see. I was a foreman of one of the crews that built the first trail around the park. It wasn't exactly what you'd call fun. We did it all by shovel and pick axe. There were no graders or steam shovels in those days. We filled in the swamps by trucking the gravel by horse and cart. At one swampy place where it looked like we were never going to get across to the other side, I said, 'O.K. As soon as this crossing is filled we're going to break off and go home no matter what time it is.' Well, all hell broke loose. You've never seen such a scramble of men, horses and sweat. The gravel was flying into that muddy gap like it was coming off a conveyor belt. They didn't even stop for lunch."

"What time did you finish?"

"Around two."

"Did you get in trouble for letting the guys off early?"

"No. In fact the engineer, an old Scotsman, wanted to make me strawboss of the whole section."

"What's a strawboss?"

"The strawboss has four foremen under him and about sixty-four men."

"Did you become a strawboss?"

"No. I refused. The strawboss needed to be able to make out timetables and pays. I didn't have any education. I couldn't do it and that's what I told MacDonald. And he said he'd get a clerk to worry about the pay if I worried about getting the road built."

"And what did you say?"

"I said I did enough worrying now. He laughed. We were the best of friends after that. I was with him right up and around Cape North. It was wild country then."

"Was that your favourite job?"

"It was interesting. I learned a lot. But it wasn't my favourite job."

"What was then?" Grandpa took off his flat cap, a smile lighting his face.

"Driving harness horses in the races at Inverness. That was my favourite job."

"That must have been great!" I said. "What was it like?" Grandfather shrugged and went back to his chopping. "What was it like, Grandpa?"

"Another time," said Grandfather.

"I'll finish the splitting after supper, I promise."

"Can't," said Grandfather.

"Why not? I don't understand."

"I can't tell you what it was like because I've never driven in a race at Inverness."

"I don't understand."

"But it would have been my favourite job," smiled Grandfather.

I propped my cold feet up against the kitchen stove and listened to the crackle and sizzle of the fire. Germaine was watching television, Grandpa dozing in his rocking chair. The rain pattered against the window pane. It was easy to doze. But I had better not. The tea biscuits had to come out in a few minutes. Ten past two to be exact. A little butter and strawberry jam and they would make a perfect afternoon snack.

The ground needed the rain. It would be good for the garden and the fields. Curious thing, to be happy about rain. I had never noticed much before what the weather was like. It didn't matter much. There were just two measures of climate in my city vocabulary. Either it was "nice out" or it wasn't. But in the country the weather became a complex companion, a companion you had to respect and understand. A stiff inshore breeze could keep the small boats from going out. Gale force winds could scatter the best laid lobster pots, smash boats and shake farm buildings. A strong, friendly sun made work a hot and sweaty affair, but ripened the crops with each passing minute. Rain at the right time complemented the sun's warm work. Rain at the wrong moment could wreck an entire year's expectations. Each morning Grandpa and I would search the broad sky. What kind of a day would it be today? Would the weather man be right? God bless him. Wrong again. Those clouds out at sea were surely rain clouds. We stuffed our sou-westers and rain jackets in the back of the cart and headed up for the summer pasture, the sun playing "catch as catch can" with each passing cloud.

"Don't you think we should hurry, Grandpa?" I asked.

"Sure, but if we go any faster the cart will bounce into pieces. If we come home early it won't be the end of the world. The job can wait for another day." But it didn't have to wait. We made it up to the summer pasture without the rain descending. Donald carefully picked his way across the pasture up the first hill and down the other side. He knew his way to the old spring as well as the cattle who followed us at some distance. It was the wooden boxing around the spring that we had come to repair. The cattle had pushed mud into the spring and the protective boxing had been broken. It was a small, low-lying spring and if the boxing were left unrepaired, the water would eventually become fouled by the cattle's feet.

"Do you want to start with the shovel?" asked Grandpa.

"Sure." I tucked my pants into my boots, grabbed a shovel and jumped down. The day was coolish, but the work wasn't easy and it soon had me in a fine sweat. Each muddy shovelful was accompanied by a great, surging, sucking sound from the spring as the clean water rushed in to replace the mud. And gradually as I worked, the water colour bubbled out from brackish to crystal. I worked on steadily until there was only gravel showing at the bottom. By that time Grandpa had the carpentry completed. We then replaced the broken boards with new ones and the spring was once more safe from marauding bovine feet. None too soon. Thunder cracked in the sky overhead. I had been too busy to notice but while we had been working the thunder clouds had darkened and meshed to close off the sky. It was difficult to believe it was only the forenoon. The cows had wisely taken shelter in the woods.

Grandfather and I hurried to get the tools put away and our rain gear on. It was no joke to be stranded in an open field during a thunder storm. But neither of us had expected the storm to blow up quite so quickly. The weatherman had called for rain showers later in the day and a storm tomorrow. A tremendous crack of lightning streaked across the sky. Donald screamed but the neigh was lost in the rumble of the thunder as it smashed above us like giant waves against some heavenly beach. Grandfather tried to quiet Donald but the big horse was being difficult, the whites of his eyes showing crazily, his huge feet prancing in short, choppy, dangerous steps. If he didn't calm down, he was going to upset the cart. I threw the last tools into the cart and prepared to hop aboard for a quick ride home.

"Clive," Grandpa hollered.

"Yes, Grandpa."

"Unhitch him. We'll never make it back in one piece in this weather. We can pick the cart up tomorrow."

"O.K.," I answered, but it was easier said than done. Even with Grandpa holding his head, Donald kept side-stepping, and everytime he sidestepped, the big horse threw the weight of the cart down onto the harness. I couldn't get a straight purchase on the shaft to thrust it upwards which would have given me the slack necessary to release the chains. Donald stopped for a second and I lifted upwards as quickly and strongly as I could. Pop. The chains came free. Now for the other side. A tremendous smash of thunder. Donald stood right up on his hind legs with Grandfather still hanging on to the bridle. I dodged as the cart steered drunkenly towards me, attached on one side to the horse. "No. Forget the cart," called Grandpa. "Unbuckle the harness!" I nodded in understanding. It was the only way, I unbuckled the harness and the belly band and Grandpa got the collar. The cart and its leather appendages finally dropped to the ground. Grandfather gathered the reins in his hands and mounted.

"Here, take my hand, Clive!" I did and somehow managed to swing on behind. Donald didn't wait for further instructions. He bolted for the pasture gate. The great horse crested the first hill at a dead gallop and then descended the other side, going faster and faster. One thing was for sure. If he stumbled we wouldn't have to worry about lightning. But Donald never faltered. He pulled up at the first gate, his sides heaving mightily. The run seemed to have calmed him. He stood still, waiting. I slipped off and opened the gate while Grandfather took him through. Once they were through, I latched it. But remounting was difficult. I didn't have the side of a hill to help me.

"Climb up on the fence post, Clive, and I'll bring him over." I nodded, but a terrible clap of thunder sent Donald into blind, cavorting circles. Grandfather reined the horse in as tightly as he could but no one in the world could have held the big chestnut at that moment.

"Go ahead, Grandpa. It's O.K. I'll walk," I yelled. Grandfather shook his head but he couldn't control Donald enough for me to mount. In pure exasperation I heard him yell, "Stay away from the trees."

"Don't worry, Grandpa. Lightning doesn't bother me," I hollered. There was no reply.

The next thunderous clap sent Donald up onto his hind legs and then horse and rider were in full flight towards the barn and I was left alone under the mighty crashing and jagged flashes of lightning. I pulled my souwester down against the spatters of rain. Nothing much though. The fast rain would come later, which was just as well. I disliked rain more than thunder. I wasn't afraid, mostly just tired. At home I had seen many electrical storms roll in over the Gatineau hills. Wrestling with the frightened horse and the morning's heavy work had left my arms and shoulders twitching with fatigue. I thought of how Grandfather's right thumb sometimes trembled slightly when he relaxed in his rocker, as if he was still lifting and sawing and banging things.

The thunder rolled and a magnificent bolt of lightning patterned the sky. I trudged on. It was about half a mile to the house. It seemed further. The sky was now completely choked with thunderheads. Quite spectacular really. It was so dark, a curious kind of darkness. Not like the coming of night. The air around me had changed from clear midday to a dense, dirty grey, as if someone had been sick inside the sky. Another tremendous smashing crash and then a solid bolt of lightning arched from cloud to earth so bright for a moment I cast a small, flickering shadow. And suddenly I realized the basic difference in my situation. I wasn't looking at the storm from the safety of a house or a car—I was in it. Cattle got killed in storms like this; so did men. There was no shelter for me at all. Nothing except for the occasional tree, the fields spread out around me flat and open. The sky lit up again in a sick, bright colour. My instincts told me to hide under a tree but Grandpa had said to avoid them. I began to run, but had to stop, my heart hammering wildly, my breath coming in great gulps. The house and barn seemed to have settled into a mirage. Never any closer. The sound of my feet came to me, swishing gently through the grass, moving like a snail. God, if one of those streaks hit me there would be no going back to Ottawa. There would be no going anywhere. I ran faster. The sky exploded directly in front of me with a shattering crack. I stopped running and lay down. The ground felt reassuring. It was damp and cold but I was less exposed. Safer. The lightning couldn't get me here. The falling rain seemed to increase. I could feel the wet soaking through my jeans and began to shiver. Couldn't stay here all day. I stood up very slowly and saw, in the distance, Grandpa coming towards me. I ran.

"You O.K.?"

I nodded and we both ran for the barn.

The next morning Grandpa and I surveyed the damage. We'd gotten off lightly. Nothing much wrong anywhere. A leak in the carriage shed roof that would have to be fixed and that was about it. The Deveaus weren't so lucky. A gaping hole had been ripped in the roof of their house. Yet this morning, it was difficult to believe the storm had happened. The sky was clear and clean. A crystal blue that reached into forever, presiding gently over a coastline of wrecked lobster pots and fishing nets. But there were no reports of anyone killed or hurt, that was the main thing.

"Would you like to go down to the beach today, Clive?"

"Sure, I'll get my swim suit."

"And a pitchfork."

"A pitchfork?"

"That's right. We're going to do some work, too."

"What kind?"

"You'll find out," said Grandfather.

"O.K." When I re-emerged from the house with my bathing suit and two large lunches, Grandfather was waiting for me. Donald was hitched to the dump cart.

"Let's go," said Grandpa and he clicked the reins. I ran to catch up but couldn't climb up with the lunches in each hand so I threw them up to Grandpa. He caught them and put them in the back. Then I climbed up. Once I was up beside him, Donald's long stride quickened into a trot and we began to jolt and crash down the lane in a bone-separating rattle, the steel rims against the gravel, kicking up a harsh cacophony of sounds.

"Couldn't we have taken the buggy?"

"Can't load seaweed into a buggy," Grandpa yelled back with a grin. I didn't try to reply. Conversation would have to wait.

Once onto the highway the noise settled down to a steady howl. Dump carts were made for fields, not roads. My bum was already going numb against the narrow wooden seat. Luckily the beach wasn't too far and as we came around the corner I could see the strip of sand curving along the edge of the sea, the waves breaking far out against another sand bar.

Grandfather didn't seem to be the only one with the idea of collecting seaweed. The beach was dotted with an odd assortment of vehicles—dump carts like ours, tractors with hitches, half-ton trucks—it seemed like everyone who did a bit of farming in the village was there. Seaweed, obviously, had an attraction that I had been unaware of. There certainly was enough of it. The storm had thrown an enormous amount of the dank, evil-smelling stuff onto the beach. Grandpa directed Donald off the highway to the side road down which we rumbled, rattled and roared to the beach.

"There's Roland and Uncle Gerard. Can we park by them, Grandpa?"

"Sure," and we pulled in slowly beside my uncle and cousin who were busy finishing off their load.

"Hi, Clive! You're late," called Roland.

"We are? There seems to be plenty of the stuff still around."

"There won't be in another hour."

"What's seaweed good for anyway."

"Puts hair on your chest," called Uncle Gerard.

"No, no," interrupted Grandpa. "Don't let him tease you, Clive. Storm seaweed attracts lobster. No one knows why, it just does."

"But we don't fish for lobster, Grandpa," I said a bit puzzled. "Will we sell it?"

"Of course," said Grandpa. "Storm seaweed must sell at what . . . two dollars a pound, eh Gerard?"

"No, no. More than that, Papa," said Uncle Gerard. "Last time I was at the Co-op I got two-fifty. It's probably up since then."

"Well, let's get loading, Grandpa. We can pick up a couple of hundred dollars easy." And I jumped down and began to fork the heavy seaweed as speedily as I could into the back of the cart. It seemed like found gold to me. Even the smell seemed to have taken on a pleasant, salty quality.

By noon we had the cart loaded right to the top of the box. Poor old Donald had to put his shoulders into it to pull the weight across the sand. It looked like we had at least two hundred dollars' worth. Uncle Gerard and Roland had already left as had most of the others. I had been so busy working I hadn't noticed the beach slowly return to a crescent of white sand stretching towards the headland.

"Want to go for a swim?" asked Grandpa.

"Another time, let's take the seaweed straight to the Co-op. Think of it—two hundred dollars," I exclaimed, the cart full of seaweed turning to gold before my eyes.

"No. Let's go home first. I'm hungry," said Grandpa.

"We've got lunch," I said. "Remember, Aunt Germaine made us some?"

"That's right. I forgot. Where did you put it?"

"Oh, no," I cried, remembering. I had been so anxious to get started. "It's at the bottom of the seaweed."

"Never mind. Let's go home."

The ride home seemed to take forever. Donald plodded and I walked most of the way. Six o'clock breakfast is a long way from twelve-thirty lunch. I was starved. Even the seaweed began to look good. Maybe the lobsters knew something we didn't. I tried a nibble but it tasted awful.

"When it dries out, it's not too bad," said Grandpa philosophically.

We finally reached our farm lane, crested the two small hills and arrived at the house.

"You go into the house, Clive."

"No, I'll help with the unharnessing," I said resolutely, abiding by the farmers' unwritten rule—horses first, people second.

"Thanks," said Grandpa. "But let's dump the fertilizer first."

"What fertilizer?" I asked puzzled.

"The seaweed," said Grandpa. "Best fertilizer you can imagine. Does amazing things for the garden."

"You mean it's not worth two-fifty a pound?"

"Mon dieu, Clive. A lobster doesn't sell for two-fifty a pound."

"You tricked me."

"It was too good an opportunity to miss. And by gosh, did you work ever fast. I've never seen anything like it," smiled Grandpa, and his smile grew into great chuckles and the chuckles into heaves and the heaves into cheery gales, until he was in a perfect paroxysm of laughter. I couldn't help but smile too. A small smile.

There was a tingle of excitement in the air. Haying time was coming close. Grandfather had both horses shod. It had cost twenty-four dollars! We were gradually getting the machinery ready. The mower had been pulled out from the machine shed, cleaned, oiled and greased. The cutting bar had been laboriously sharpened, each wedge-shaped tooth carefully hand filed and the loose ones replaced. The square box was taken off the timber truck and the hayrack was lowered slowly from the barn rafters until it rested on the frame of the truck where we latched it down. It certainly looked like a noble wagon, with four, broad, flat fenders over each wheel and a tall frame at each end; but I couldn't for the life of me figure out how it was going to hold the hay because there was nothing along the sides but thin air. Nevertheless I admired the hayrack Grandpa had built and kept my ignorance to myself. I was learning to wait. To me all the farm machinery looked mysterious.

Grandfather had engaged David Boudreau to help with the harvest, as well as another man. Aunt Germaine was planning for the large meals she would soon be serving at lunch break. Now all that remained was to wait for the right moment to begin. The fine weather continued and one by one our neighbours swung into the frantic activity of haying. Uncle Gerard had started. Then in quick succession the Chiassons, the Cormiers, the LeBlancs until it seemed we were the only ones in the whole parish who hadn't begun. I didn't understand it. Why were we so late to begin the most important harvest on the farm calendar? It wasn't like Grandfather. Each morning we would make a careful survey of the hayfields. And I would pester him.

"Can't we start today, Grandpa? The weather's fine."

"Yes, it is," said Grandfather with a quick smile. "It's mighty tempting but I don't think we'll start just yet. Maybe at the end of the week."

"But why? Everyone else has started."

"That's their decision. Maybe it's right for their hayfields. But I don't think we're quite ready yet. The hay needs another week."

"Why? I don't understand. Roland says the longer you wait to cut the grass, the less 'heart' there is to it."

"That's true, but your crop is bigger if you wait. I guess it's a balance you want to strike. I prefer the heavy side of the balance."

"Don't worry about the cows," laughed Grandpa. "They'll get their vitamins."

"From what?" I smiled, picturing in my mind Grandpa administering cod liver oil to each cow during the winter.

"From turnips. Not too many farmers bother with them any more but they pay their way."

"What about rain? The weather's fine now. It might not be next week."

"Then we're in trouble. But I can't do anything about that. God deals the cards. I just play them the best way I know how. You know who used to say that?"

"No."

"Nor do I," Grandpa laughed. "But we shouldn't have to worry. The weatherman has called for good weather right to the end of July."

I groaned. The only thing right about our weatherman was that he was always wrong. I didn't know how Grandpa could stay so calm. We had three beautiful hayfields over forty acres, and they showed the years of careful tending by our family. There wasn't another farm in the parish that was blessed with such thick, rich grass. The timothy was waist high and moved in deep, green waves all the way from the foot of the summer pasture to the cliffs above the sea. I looked up at Grandpa and could see he was really proud too. "We'll start soon," he said gruffly. "But today we've got other work to do."

"What's that?"

"Run the cultivator over the turnips and the potatoes," said Grandfather dryly.

"Oh," I said disappointed because that usually meant I mainly sat and watched.

"Let's use both cultivators. It'll go more quickly that way."

"You'll trust me to drive a cultivator all alone?"

"Sure. Just remember to watch Nellie's feet as well as the cultivator blade."

I was surprised and flattered. It was tricky work driving a horse and at the same time guiding the cultivator between the long rows of turnips. A false turn and you could rip out the growing vegetables instead of the weeds, which is exactly what I had done the last time I had tried it. Turnips were an important crop to Grandfather. In Cape Breton the growing season is usually too short for corn, so instead Grandfather grew turnips, which are a much hardier vegetable. All you had to do was make sure they had a fighting chance against weeds and bugs. Then in the late fall when other work was slow, the turnips were harvested. They were used as silage for the cattle, just as Ontario farmers used corn. Hay and turnip silage—a curious mixture, but they worked well for our cattle. I hummed a little to myself as I went down to the barn to put the harness on the horses.

David Boudreau

The steady whir of the cutting bar dominated the still, hot day. Our haying had begun, the tall grass coming down neatly to the ground, as the horses strained into their harness. Cutting hay was the toughest work I had ever seen Nellie and Donald do. The cutting bar was driven by the rotating wheels of the mower so the horses had not only to pull a rather heavy machine, but also provide the power to bring the grass down. It was heavy, continuous work that once begun couldn't be delayed. As long as the weather was fine you had to grind on. The two old horses had done it many times before and they knew the routine, heads down, pulling steadily, evenly. A grand team, they moved forward together step by step, with never a falter, like the old pros they were. But by mid-morning old Nellie was labouring more than she should have been. I was kind of worried about her. She seemed to be really struggling to keep up with her partner, her distended sides caked in white lather. It must have been on Grandfather's mind also because he stopped the mower and called to me, "Clive, can you run over to Gerard's and see if we can borrow his horse for this afternoon? I don't think Nellie's going to make it through the whole day." And he made a sign with his arms to indicate her distended middle. I nodded and set off for Gerard's place immediately.

It turned out as Grandpa had hoped. Uncle Gerard was using a tractor, a baling machine, and the like for his haying. His one remaining horse, a big grey-speckled fellow called Bill, was decorating a rough pasture by the sea along with a few cows. He watched me approach, strong and very full of himself. He kicked up his heels, and galloped to the other end of the pasture, not interested in my small bucket of oats and not at all fooled. He certainly was a powerful fellow, squat and built like a tank—quite different from the more rangy Clydesdales that Nellie and Donald drew their parentage from. I began to walk towards him once more rattling the bucket invitingly. Suddenly he turned and came charging straight towards me. My throat went dry. "I should have come out with Roland," was the one thought that flashed through my mind before the thundering monster stopped a few short yards in front of me. Then he advanced slowly and buried his head like a lamb in the bucket of oats. Once he had got a good start on the oats, I reached up for his halter. He didn't jump and I began to lead him cautiously to the barn. He came quietly, but I could feel the tensed spring in his step. If we could ever get this fellow hitched up, he was going to give old Donald a run for his money.

"Hi, Clive." I turned to see my cousin, Roland. "Need a hand?"

"No, I've got the bridle on. Anything I should know about him before I take him over to Grandpa's?"

"Just one thing. He kicks when you hitch him up to anything. Doesn't like to work much. Dad's going to sell him. Myself, I don't think you'll be able to use him."

"Maybe Grandpa will think of something. He's good with horses."

"O.K., but remember to warn him," advised Roland again.

"How about riding? Does he buck or anything like that?" I asked nervously.

"No, but he'll probably try and take the bit in his mouth

and run." I looked at the big grey horse in bewilderment. It had never occurred to me that other horses might be different. Nellie and Donald were so well behaved.

"Don't worry Clive. You're right. Grandpa will probably settle him down. Dad says Grandpa speaks three languages—French, English and horse."

"That's fine, but in the meantime I'm liable to get killed."

"You can ride him, don't worry. Just run the devil out of him right at the start. That's what I do." Then he turned to go.

"Aren't you staying to watch the action?"

"No, I've got to get back."

"How's your haying coming along?"

"With luck we'll be finished by the middle of next week. Dad's promised to take me down to Chéticamp Beach on Sunday. Want to come?"

"Sure."

"O.K. See you around two."

"Easy for you to say," I said. Roland grinned and left me with Bill. We eyed each other appraisingly. I don't know who was more uneasy, the huge horse or me. Well, I had no choice. Old Nellie needed him. I eased onto his bare back from the porch railing. I could feel his muscles jumping underneath my legs like live wires. There was no question in my mind and less in Bill's—the second I gave him the chance, he was going to take off like an express train. I reined in on the bit until my arms ached, but he still sidestepped in something between a canter and a trot all the way down the lane. Things didn't look too promising for a safe journey home. There was a lot more of him than there was of me. At that moment, I'd settle for doing just as Roland had advised—point him in the right direction and hang on.

We turned the corner onto the highway. Bill was losing patience with the tight rein. I could feel it. He threw up his hind legs in a play-buck and I smashed my nose adroitly against the back of his neck. Bill didn't seem to notice but I did. I felt dizzy and slightly sick. Some blood dripped down on my trousers. I wiped my nose with my shirtsleeve, at the same time easing up on the reins. The big horse didn't miss the opportunity and sprang immediately into a tremendous headlong charge, his mane snapping into my face. The roadside flying along beneath me, sparks cracking up between his steel shoes and the pavement. I tried not to think about falling off onto the asphalt. The farm drew near. I pulled up on the reins. No response. I pulled up a little harder—no response. The big horse thundered on. Bill had the bit firmly clenched in his teeth. I was strictly a passenger. Grandfather watched from the mower as the big grey horse galloped all the way down to the Co-op where he began to slow down and finally loosened the bit from his teeth. I didn't waste the moment. I wheeled him around and we galloped back, considerably slower, towards the farm. Grandfather had the mower parked beside the barn and was in the process of unhitching the horses when we finally arrived.

"What happened?"

"Horse ran away with me."

"You O.K.?"

"Fine."

"How's the horse?"

"Sound, but crazy as a hoot. Roland says he kicks when you hitch him up." I slipped off the horse. Grandfather shrugged.

"What can you expect? He's a young horse and no one's ever taught him any manners. Can you take Donald and Nellie down to the stable and I'll see if I can fix something up for this young fellow?"

"Sure." I hurried the two old comrades down to their stalls, anxious to return and see what Grandfather was going to do. The old mare eased up to her manger with a sigh of relief.

When I got back, Grandfather had a pair of shafts hitched up to absolutely nothing at all. Just two shafts sitting on two barrels but the grey horse was all harnessed up as if he was going to pull something, somewhere.

"What's up?" I asked.

"We'll see in a minute," said Grandfather enigmatically. Then Grandpa backed up the grey horse between the two shafts. Nothing happened. "Try hitching him up," said Grandfather. "Stay well to the side." I nodded and, feeling somewhat foolish, proceeded to hitch his harness to the shafts. The big hind-quarters exploded in a devastating double kick but as the horse's feet met with absolutely no resistance, his legs extended more fully than he intended. His back hooves hung in the air for a second. The horse seemed to shudder with the effort of drawing them back under him, unbalanced and slowly fell forward onto his knees. For a moment he lay sprawled among the barrels and shafts before he stood up, unhurt but shaking and frightened.

"O.K.," said Grandpa, patting him gently on the neck. "Kick all you want, young fellow. We've got plenty of time. Let's unhitch him again, Clive." We unhitched him. "O.K., hitch him up on your side." We hitched both sides of the harness to the phony wagon once more. The young horse trembled a little around the hind end as we hitched him but he didn't kick. Grandpa smiled happily and said, "He'll do." We tethered him on the mow floor on a loose rein with a little hay to keep him occupied, and went to lunch.

The fresh smell of baking cinnamon rolls wafted toward us as we opened the porch door. Mmmm. The smell was delicious. I took off my boots with lightning-fast speed and seated myself at the kitchen table. No announcement was needed. The competing sights and smells from the stove announced to us dinner was ready. The table was laid very simply. There were no frills—just plates, knives and forks sedately set on a checkered oil-cloth. But both Grandfather and I knew a very fine meal awaited us. Aunt Germaine began the meal by serving some thick clam chowder. I helped myself to some fresh bread and butter. The chowder was delicious, every morsel, and then with scarcely taking a break, we moved on to the main course—baked potatoes, peas, beans and slices of home-cured ham. Grandfather turned on the radio and we listened for the news and weather before sampling some of Germaine's golden-brown cinnamon rolls. I groaned and leaned back from the table, content and very full. It was most definitely nap time.

"Clive," said Grandfather. "Could you do something for me this afternoon?"

"Sure."

"Go over to David Boudreau's and see if he can begin with us tomorrow."

"Why not phone him?"

"Because he doesn't have a phone. Doesn't believe in it," said Grandfather.

"He might have to work then," sniffed Aunt Germaine.

"I suppose that's it," said Grandfather comfortably and he took his slim frame, with a definite waddle, over to the rocking chair. "Can you go over, Clive . . . after your nap?"

"And dishes," said Aunt Germaine.

"And dishes?" I said.

"Did you know David used to be a beau of Germaine's?" asked Grandpa with a smile.

"Along with every other girl in the village," replied Aunt Germaine.

"He's still unmarried," said Grandfather. There was a short silence while Aunt Germaine and I got the dishes underway.

"Oh, David is a fine fellow," said my aunt quietly. "Just never had much of a head for anything but stories."

"Where exactly does he live?" I asked.

"You know the road that goes up towards the Salt Pond from the old schoolhouse?"

"Yes."

"Well, it's the little green house back from the road."

We finished the dishes and I tumbled onto the couch, bone-tired and thoroughly happy. At that moment I couldn't have explained why. At a time when most of my friends had been shipped off to camp to learn recreational skills, I was working each day. It began at the crack of six with milking and, except for lunch break, Grandpa and I worked right through to six in the evening. With haying time having arrived, it would be even later. But the long hours didn't bother me. I loved the work. The early afternoon sun streamed in through the window, warming the room pleasantly, and soon I was sound asleep.

Looking back I guess I know another reason why I felt so happy. In Ottawa we lived in a rented house. The family shuttled around the country following my father's career. I didn't really know what he did. It was something to do with economics and fish. His work kept him very busy, on the move, and it kept his children adapting to new schools, new neighbourhoods and new friends. In the village I didn't have to explain myself or my funny name. I was *Clive à Fernand à William Arsène*—Clive, the son of Fernand, the son of William Arsène. I could feel the roots of the family Doucet. They went down deep into the earth and into the community. It was a comforting feeling to know I was living in the same house my father had grown up in, to be walking across the same fields, going to the same church—these simple acts filled a void inside me that had been growing wider and wider with every urban move the family made.

Grandfather always had time for a multitude of joys—

to teach me the crafts of farming, to tell me stories and, best of all, to be my Grandpa.

David Boudreau's house was more of a cabin than a house. A clapboard miniature. It didn't look like it had more than two rooms. Its humility looked a little intimidating. The cabin was set back from the road in what had once been a very large pasture but was quickly changing to scrub bush. A pile of timbers indicated where a barn of some sort had once stood. A wide, grassy pathway had been scythed from the road to the house. I walked up to the door and knocked gently. A ferocious barking greeted me. I very nearly jumped out of my skin with surprise. Very few people kept dogs in the parish because of the sheep and because of the habit dogs had of chasing them off cliffs or into barbed-wire fences with cheery canine glee.

I was looking about for a handy tree to climb in case the animal behind the door got loose, when the door swung open, and a friendly human face emerged, a pipe in one hand, the dog held by the other hand.

"Good day," he said and smiled.

"Good day," I said. "How are you Mr. Boudreau?"

"Just fine," said David Boudreau, and his infectious smile grew broader.

"And how is Clive Doucet?"

"Fine, thank you, sir."

"Just a minute, I'll get some chairs. We'll sit outside. It's too nice to be inside today." Mr. Boudreau released the straining dog and disappeared back into the house while what looked like a collie shot by me and up the road. A few seconds later David Boudreau emerged with two chairs. He was a huge man—towering above me, barrel-chested with a copious pot belly that spread handsomely along, but not over, his belt. A very different fellow from my Grandfather who was a little on the elfish side, fine-boned and quite small. You would have thought they came from separate planets, except for their hands. David Boudreau's were much like Grandfather's, large, muscled and capable.

"Your dog's gone," I noted a little foolishly. But Mr. Boudreau puffed on his pipe and didn't seem concerned. "Not a sheep chaser, then," I said trying to make conversation.

"Never touches sheep. Too smart for that, Clive. In fact I've been told he's the smartest dog in the whole country. . . ." After some pipe smoking and reflection, ". . . some say he's the smartest dog on the whole island, maybe in the whole province . . . maybe in the whole country."

"Must be a pretty smart dog," I said, cleverly figuring that was what I was expected to say.

"Well some people don't believe me when I tell them how smart my dog is."

"Why not?" I asked faithfully. David Boudreau leaned back on his chair and puffed a little more on his pipe, considering the matter. "Well, that collie of mine is so smart, he can tell time. Can you believe that?" Acting in the spirit of things, I considered the pros and cons of the situation for a few moments before opting for a compromise response.

"It does seem a bit difficult to believe, Mr. Boudreau. But you must remember I don't know much about dogs. We don't have one either at home or here."

"I see," said Mr. Boudreau, nodding understandingly. "Most people around here are in the same boat—don't know a damn thing about dogs either, but they'd never admit it." He reflected and puffed some more, considering the angle of the sun and what not. "They didn't believe me either when I told them my dog could tell time. So you know what I did?"

"No."

"I invited some of my neighbours over for a demonstration. If I remember, your Uncle Armand was in the crowd." Uncle Armand was now, conveniently, in Montreal.

"What happened?" I asked.

"Well, I used to keep some cows in the field behind the house. I don't any more because I'm getting on. (David Boudreau couldn't have been more than fifty then, thirty years younger than Grandpa.) My dog would come into the house, look at the clock and, once the hands hit four o'clock, off he'd go to get the cows. If you can imagine, I had six people crowded in my little kitchen, everyone waiting, including the dog, for my clock to strike four. Then you know what happened?"

"No," I said.

"I turned the clock face against the wall so that no one could see the time. Can you guess what happened then?"

"No."

"The poor dog began to pace around the room, sniffing here and there, obviously very distressed, but I wouldn't relent. He jumped up at my chest and looked at the clock, begging for me to turn it around so that he could see the time. Then he tried everyone else in the room but I forbade anyone to turn the clock face around. Well you should have seen my poor old dog. He was going ill with pure frustration, whining and crying. Finally he ran outside and in a fit of desperation shaded his eyes with his paw and looked at the sun. Then with a happy bark and a wag of the tail he ran off to get the cows. Well, everyone had been so busy watching his antics they had all forgotten about the clock but when I turned the face of the clock around, it was right on four o'clock, just like I knew it would be—isn't that something?"

Before I could agree or disagree, the hero of the story came racing around the corner, a farmer in hot pursuit behind him. "David Boudreau, keep your damn dog tied up! He's been devillin' my wife's chickens."

"You must have mistaken him for some other dog," smiled David indulgently. "My dog's too smart for that." From under his master's chair, the smartest dog in all of Canada thumped his tail in complete agreement. While the farmer and David settled down to some serious arguing, I listened for some time and then left. Neither men noticed. I had the feeling they were both enjoying themselves.

"Did David say he would be over tomorrow?" called Grandfather to me over the noise of the mowing machine. I nodded to indicate "yes," rather than try and compete with the noise of the machine. Grandpa waved and the hot work went on. Donald and Bill didn't match very well—one a golden chestnut, the other a silver-grey; one rangy, the other bulky. But they worked well together. The older horse steadied the younger one, while Bill helped Donald with some much needed pulling power. In the meantime Nellie swanned around the night pasture keeping quietly out of sight while her compatriots kept working until the grass began to dampen with dew.

It was two very large and very tired horses I led to the stables that night. To my surprise Grandfather was already snoozing in his rocker by the time I returned to the house. It was only eight o'clock. Usually we played checkers or something. I shouldn't have been surprised. Grandpa was seventy-eight years old and he had just spent almost ten hours bouncing around a baking-hot hayfield. But at twelve, twenty years old tends to blend into thirty and fifty into seventy. There doesn't seem to be that much difference.

The next morning dawned bright and clear with no hint of rain on the horizon—just a few ragged clouds here and there scuttling along high in the sky. Grandfather continued with the relentless work of cutting hay and I began to turn the rows of hay over so that they would dry better in the sun. It was hot, slow work and I was all alone, the sound of the mowing machine just a distant hum. I wondered where David Boudreau was. He was supposed to be here to help this morning as was one of Gilles Deveau's older boys, but no one had showed up.

It felt kind of lonely and futile. There was no way I could turn all this hay by myself. It was thick and matted. While the top portion had already begun to whiten, it was still green and grassy underneath. The flat hay needed to be turned but the job was so big and my pitchfork so small. For the first time on the farm I began despairing. What was the point? I was only me. I might as well have had a kitchen fork in my hands for all the chance I had of working methodically across the entire field. The sun's heat bounced off the cut grass and onto my chest and face as if off a mirror. Not much fun. I leant on my pitchfork desultorily and wondered what the time was. I felt a prickly heat rash on the back of my neck. Damn, it was hot. I looked again across the vast expanse of field and up to the sky. I might as well be a mouse. No, a mouse wouldn't see the sky quite from this angle. It would be more from the ground. I lay down, my back against the mattress of baking grass. This is more the perspective a mouse would have. From here the sky didn't look like the sky at all, just a vacant dimensionless blue. Kind of scary. No wonder mice spent so much of their time underground. If there was a cloud or something to give the blueness an edge, or a corner, or a centre, or something. As if on order, a small cloud came into sight, a small, white, fluffy cloud. It blinked out the sun for a moment and then continued on its way across the sky. A baby cloud. I wondered if it was lost.

"There is a lost cloud reported at the Inverness County

sky desk. Would the parents of Baby Cloud 3947 please report to the Cape Breton area for a banana-cream pie fight. Otherwise go directly to Africa."

Perhaps if I put a little hay over my face, I would get a better view of the mouse perspective on African and Cape Breton clouds—and that was the last thing I remembered before drifting off into sleep.

"Giddap there, Donald! Giddap! What's the matter?" The sound of Grandfather's voice woke me. I looked up through the hay covering me to see the underside of Donald's and Bill's bridles. Definitely an unusual view of our esteemed team. Then it occurred to me that their steel-shod hooves were parked about a foot from my naked head. I rolled out of the way and stood up, trying to shake the hay off and the dizzy feeling from standing up too quickly.

"Clive! My God, are you all right?"

"Yes, I'm fine," I said calmly, a bit confused. Then Grandpa jumped down from the mowing machine. He seemed to be shaking.

"Are you sure you're all right?"

"Sure, fine. Didn't you see me?"

"No," said Grandpa, still trembling, whereupon he cracked me across the side of the head with the flat of his hand so hard I staggered, lost my balance and fell down. "Don't you ever, ever, ever lie down in a field where machines are working again! Understand me! . . . Understand?"

"Yes, Grandpa."

"Where's David and Gilles?"

"They didn't show up."

"Must be my lucky day," said Grandpa thickly. "You go to the house and clean up. Don't say a word about this to Germaine. She has enough to worry about, understand?"

"Yes, Grandpa." I set off across the field towards the

house. Was the cutting bar up or down? I couldn't remember. I shut the porch door behind me quietly, took my boots off and began to wash up.

"How did you make out?" asked Aunt Germaine.

"It was slow." I said trying hard to keep a calm edge to my voice. "Neither David Boudreau nor Gilles showed up."

"I know," said Aunt Germaine. "Gilles phoned. He's still working at the LeVert's. Their harvest is taking longer than expected and David's got a cold."

"What was that?" asked Grandfather entering the kitchen.

"Gilles is still at the LeVert's and David's got a cold."

"A cold? Like hell. More like an allergy—to work."

We ate our lunch in unaccustomed silence. I was still pre-occupied with my close escape. The magnitude of our harvest problem hadn't really settled clearly in my mind. Grandpa and I did everything else on the farm. Why not do the entire hay harvest by ourselves too? Then I thought of the size of just ten acres of cut hay and my heart sank. We couldn't do it. Somehow all that hay had to be turned. It would take me three days at least. It had to be done in a day. Grandpa must also have been thinking along the same lines because he said, "Clive, this afternoon you get the hay rake. Use Nellie. I want you to rake the hay into very thin rows. It will be harder to cock but the effect will be to turn the hay as well as prepare it."

"For what?"

"For loading."

"But you can't do it alone," said Aunt Germaine quietly.

"Why don't I go up to Chiassons' place this evening," I asked. They seem to be about finished their haying. Maybe Joe could help us?" Grandpa nodded in absent-minded agreement. I wasn't sure he had heard me.

We finished lunch and went straight back to work.

Nellie squeezed herself in between the shafts of the hay rake and we ambled off. The hay rake turned out to be a simple but very effective device. Basically it was a large spring-loaded comb held between two wheels. The spring held the comb down. When you wanted to raise the comb and drop the gathered hay, you simply punched a lever with the heel of your boot and the comb popped up, releasing the hay. Then the spring brought the comb back to earth once more. It was light work. Easy as pie. I just had to keep on going until it was done. By supper time most of the field was raked into even rows. Now all we had to do was find someone to help us load the hay.

After a quick supper Grandpa set off to see David Boudreau. With a couple of cinnamon rolls tucked in my sweater, I too set off in search of help. It was a beautiful summer evening, a warm summer sunset splashing across the sea. The Chiassons' little house sat snuggled up against the mountains like a fairy-tale cottage surveying the universe from a position of authority. In spite of the quiet lustre of the evening, I sure didn't feel like making the long walk across the fields to the Chiassons' place. But there was little choice. All three horses needed time to recover from the long day's work.

As I climbed towards the Chiassons' farm, gradually the whole parish came into view. From the cluster of buildings at the harbour, the houses and farms cascaded along the coastline, dotting it with bright pastel colours. I wondered if our little church had grace. The priest had said last Sunday that two of the cornerstones of the Catholic Church were mystery and grace. The church was a white clapboard building, its back was towards the sea, the spire and front door facing the parish and the mountains. Words like isolated, pretty, defiant came easily to mind, but not grace. That word was more difficult to deal with. Grace was something you achieved through ceremonious practice. I wondered if the cinnamon roll that I was munching on had grace or the evening I was walking in. They certainly seemed to.

I climbed the fences which surrounded the Chiassons' garden. The sun was just sinking into the sea's horizon. Except for that distant glow, it was quite dark and I trod my way carefully along the edge of the well-tended garden.

"Clive, is that you?" Joe's voice called.

"It's myself," I called back and then entered the warm kitchen and seated myself beside Joe. Mrs. Chiasson put the kettle on and brought out some gingerbread cookies.

"Try some of these," she ordered cheerfully.

"Thanks." As I reached out for a cookie, my hand trembled slightly. I regarded it curiously, as if it was attached to someone else's body. The cookie felt small and very delicate in the palm of my hand.

"Some tea?" asked Mrs. Chiasson, as she poured me a cup.

"Yes, please." I sipped the hot tea cautiously, cruel experience having taught me that tea in Grand Etang only came one way—just a degree or so off the boil. But the scalding drink worked and in spite of the fatigue, I began to perk up.

Anne sat down next to Joe on the other side of the table.

"What happened to your face, Clive?"

"Ask my mother," I shrugged, a bit defensive at her gentle, penetrating stare.

"It's burnt," said Joe and he fetched a small mirror. I looked in the mirror. Nothing seemed amiss—a tanned, freckled face, broad nose, brown eyes—the face I usually saw when I looked in the mirror. Then I noticed it—a bright, red streak of sunburn across my forehead.

"Oh, that," I said, sheepishly. "I fell asleep in the field this morning. I guess I didn't have my cap on."

"You fell asleep," laughed Joe. "Some guys have it easy! Want to trade jobs? You help up here and I'll help your grandad with his haying."

"Actually, I was kind of hoping you could spare the time, Joe. Grandpa and I need the help. Both men who were going to help us haven't shown up. So there's just me and Grandpa."

"Just you and William to do the whole farm?" exclaimed Mr. Chiasson, entering the kitchen from the living room. "Is that right?"

"Yes, sir."

"Damn. That's ridiculous. You and the old man can't do it alone."

"It is hard. I was wondering if you could give us a hand—when you're finished."

"But we won't be finished for another seven or eight days. Most evenings I'm working at the fish plant. I can't spare Joe or Pierre or. . . ." Mr. Chiasson turned towards the stove and began tapping his pipe against the grate before turning back to me. "What about Gerard? Can't he help?"

"I think. . . ." I let the sentence trail off, unsure how to complete it.

"What?" asked Joe.

"Grandpa won't ask Uncle Gerard."

"Why? He's got a tractor . . . machines."

"Pride, I guess."

"But Gerard's his son!" exclaimed Mrs. Chiasson.

"I think that's why," I said slowly. There was an embarrassed silence for a few moments.

"Gerard would help," said Mr. Chiasson. I stirred my tea, uncertain as to how I should reply. Uncle Gerard had his trucking business to look after, his own haying to do. Last winter he brought Grandpa his furnace wood. Uncle Gerard would help, he was that kind of person, but Grandpa wasn't ever going to ask him. I just knew he wouldn't. I nodded towards Mr. Chiasson, as if agreeing, and drank my tea down quickly.

Anne and Joe were joking about something. Then Joe said, "Are you playing ball Sunday afternoon in Chéticamp, Clive?"

"Sure, if we're not working."

"Well if you're not, you get a drive with us."

"O.K. Thanks very much and thanks for the tea and gingerbread, Mrs. Chiasson. They were delicious." I stood up. "Guess I'd better get going. Long day tomorrow."

"I'll help," said Anne.

"Pardon?"

"I will help the Doucets."

"What about your job at the Co-op?" asked Mrs. Chiasson.

"Marie can come in for the week or so I'm away. She's anxious to try."

"It's pretty hard work," I said dubiously, regarding Anne's slim frame.

"Anne can make hay as well as you can," said Mr. Chiasson gently. I could feel my face flushing red. What a dumb thing for me to have said.

"What time do you start?" asked Anne, undisturbed by my foolishness.

"As soon as the dew is burned off," I said, feeling a strange tightening in my chest.

As I left, the moon lighted my way home, the sky bright and sparkling with summer stars. It seemed only a few moments before I was walking directly towards the soft, yellow light of our own porch.

Grandfather greeted me with a wry smile and raised his tea mug to me in a mock salute.

"Would you believe it? That old goat Boudreau really does have a cold. I ended up making him tea and tucking him in bed. Doesn't that beat all!"

Haying

Anne, Grandfather, and I. The three of us strung out along the rows of hay, each working silently, alone, insulated from one another by the summer heat, a shimmering curtain that radiated between us from both the sky and the ground. Yet the next instant it seemed we were as close to each other as three people could possibly be, each driven by a common purpose, the field of neatly piled hay testimony to our endeavours.

The handle of the pitchfork chafed against the palm of my hand. This afternoon I wouldn't be so stupid. I'd wear gloves like Anne and Grandfather.

Mr. Chiasson had been right. Anne did work well. She moved the pitchfork with an easy, practiced sweep that required only the minimum of exertion, yet allowed the maximum of return. I kept up with her only by dint of unrelenting effort. The bruises on my hand hurt (and so did my ego). Grandfather had said that this was the worst part of haying. Everything else was easy by comparison. I tried to comfort myself with this thought but my arms ached and my legs trembled slightly as I finished another *meule*. Maybe he was right. It couldn't get much worse. Don't stop—that was the key. If I stopped, I'd never get started again. I'd fall off my pitchfork and go spinning off into a large hole in the ground. And who would I meet there? Probably my father who would ask me why I was goofing off. "Clive, my son," he would say to me. "You're never going to get anywhere daydreaming. If you spent half as much time on your homework as you do daydreaming, you wouldn't be failing at school."

"Yes, Dad."

"You can't get anywhere in life without an education."

"Yes, Dad."

"Talents are God-given. It's a sin to waste them."

"Yes, Dad. Dad?"

"Yes?"

"Can you tell me just one thing?"

"I'll try."

"What are we doing in this hole?"

"We live here. We all live here. And it's not a hole. Don't you ever let me hear you say that again! *Comprends?*"

"Sorry." And I tramped off down the burrow to my room. Homework. Grandfather's voice interrupted my thoughts.

"Clive, stop! You can't do the entire field by yourself."

"Sorry," I said automatically.

"Sorry? What's there to be sorry for? You're doing fine. Let's go for lunch."

"Already?"

"It may be 'already' for you," said Anne dryly, "but for me it's 'finally.' Let's go. I'm starved."

"Sure," I said grinning. "Let's go." And we shouldered our pitchforks and headed towards the house.

"Did you ever see the likes of this lad, Anne?" asked Grandfather jokingly. Anne did not reply. "One day he may even be able to keep up with you." Anne grinned and I did not know what to say. In dungarees and a straw hat, Anne seemed more wonderful than she should be.

After lunch we pitchforked hay from the *meules* onto the wagon. Anne stayed in the wagon squaring the hay, Grandfather and I pitching from either side. When it came my turn to work on top of the wagon, it took me a while to get the hang of spreading the loose hay to the edges. Instinctively, I dragged it to the centre, but gradually I realized that it wasn't going to fall off if I spread it from the centre towards the edge. The idea was to shake the hay across the hayrack so that it formed a kind of blanket across the top. In this way, depending on how clever you were at "making the load," you could triple or quadruple the amount of hay the wagon could carry. The wagon of hay grew and grew until Grandfather and Anne were pitching the hay straight over their heads to me and I was reaching down with my pitchfork to pull the hay up. It was really quite impressive. I was quite ready to go on building the load until Donald and Bill were pulling on their knees.

Once we were in the barn I envisaged that we would have to pitch all our carefully packed hay up into the hay mow, a job that would be much harder than loading it in the field. But there was a steel device called the hay fork which didn't look like a fork at all, but more like a clumsy spear with one mechanical barb. I had never noticed it before but winter and summer it hung from a track which ran just under the roof of the barn. Once we had the hay wagon safely sitting on the mow floor, the hay fork was lowered and pushed into the top of the load, the barb snapped into place and from below Anne directed Donald who pulled the fork back up to the rafters, a great mass of hay clenched firmly in its single barb. Grandfather waited until the fork had slid along the track and the hay hung perilously over the empty mow. He then pulled a lever attached by a rope to the hayfork. Released, the hay fell five stories straight down into the empty mow. I looked down into the cavernous hole, the hay covering a tiny spot at the bottom. Five stories of empty space to fill on this side; three on the other side. It hadn't occurred to me before what an astonishing amount of hay we had to cut and truck over the next two weeks.

"Clive!" Grandpa called from the top of the mow.

"Yes, Grandpa."

"Could you go to the house and see if there's any lemonade?"

"Sure. I'll be back in a moment." It was only when the cool shade of the kitchen embraced me that I realized the back of my shirt was soaked with perspiration.

"How is it going?" asked Aunt Germaine.

"Very well, as far as I can see. We should be able to finish the bottom half of the front field today."

"Sounds fine. Here's the lemonade. Take these too," and she handed me a tin of cookies.

"Thanks. Any change. . . ."

"No change in the weather," smiled Germaine. "You're getting as bad as Papa. Why bother? You can't do anything to stop the rain anyway."

"But you can worry more," I said. "That always helps."

"If it did," sighed Germaine "we'd have sunshine twenty-four hours a day."

"Like Florida," I said.

"Like Florida," said Germaine. "Now, scoot. Be careful. And bring the jug and tin back on your way out to the field."

Each evening, right after the last load of hay had been carefully tucked away in the belly of the barn, I would drive Anne home in the buggy. We would clip-clop up the back lane, then across service road number four and down the driveway to her place. It took about the same time as walking—about twenty minutes. I always wished it took longer and sometimes Nellie would oblige. We didn't say much. Anne was a quiet girl, whereas I was a twelve-year-old dinner party, often talking on four channels about four discrete subjects simultaneously. Anne didn't bother to talk just to hear the sound of her voice;

that characteristic unnerved me more than anything else about her. She thought things through from beginning to end, mulled them over in a way that was thoroughly alarming. Her questions, answers, everything about her was carefully considered. I knew from the first time I met her at the Co-op that she was the kind of girl who held firm opinions. Once she had made up her mind about something, there was no going back. Like her decision to help Grandfather and me with the haying. Anne didn't have a robust frame. She was quite slim. But she could always be depended upon. Her will made up for what she lacked in strength. Often, especially on the first few nights, we would travel in a rather shy silence, both enjoying the end of day but unsure how to deal with the situation of being alone. On this occasion it was Anne who broke the silence.

"Clive, what do you want to be when you grow up?"

"I don't know."

"Really? Have you no idea at all?"

"I guess I do, but you'd laugh."

"No, I wouldn't. Tell me!"

"I'd like to be a farmer like Grandpa," and to my astonishment Anne replied,

"You'd make a good farmer."

I was thrilled and at the same time puzzled at Anne's flat approval of me.

"But I guess I'll never be one."

"Why not?"

"Another one of my daydreams. That's what my dad would say."

Anne considered this for a moment, her face still.

"I don't see why," she said finally. "Your grandfather has a good farm. Does anyone want it in your family?"

"No one," I said.

"Then why so glum?"

"No one wants it because these days a little farm like

Grandpa's doesn't pay. You need tractors and balers and all that modern machinery."

"Buy them then," said Anne.

"It's not that simple," I sighed. "If you buy all that machinery you need a farm four or five times the size of Grandpa's. Machines cost a lot more than horses."

"Your Uncle Gerard's got a lot of machinery," she said reasonably.

"He rents it out most of the time," I replied. "And he runs his trucks. Uncle Gerard is more of a mechanic and businessman than a farmer."

"And you're not a mechanic," smiled Anne.

"Or a businessman," I said flatly. "If it hasn't got four feet I don't know how it works. Right, Nellie?" The old mare pricked up her ears at the sound of my voice and then seeing I wasn't going to pursue the matter, relaxed once more. "What about you, Anne? What are you going to be?"

"A teacher," said Anne without hesitation.

"A teacher." I repeated a bit bewildered. "Where . . . here?"

"Probably. Why should I go elsewhere?"

"No reason, I guess. As long as there are kids to teach."

"There'll always be children," smiled Anne.

The conversation was getting a little dangerous so I concentrated on my driving which took no concentration at all, but it kept my eyes occupied.

"And fish," said Anne almost to herself.

"Pardon?"

"Children and fish. Maybe the farms will go, like you say, Clive. But there will always be fish in the ocean and as long as there are, fishermen will be needed."

"And teachers for their children," I said lightly and passed the reins over to Anne before jumping down to open the gate which opened onto number four. Anne drove the buggy through and I closed the gate behind her. By the looks of Nellie's middle, she wasn't far from foaling. It made me a bit nervous to be out with her but Grandpa had said it was all right.

"Clive, will you give me a call when Nellie foals?" asked Anne.

"Sure. It's going to be quite an event," I said. "Grandpa says when the foal arrives we should charge admission. But for you we've got a special discount!" Anne laughed.

"I'll pay. I feel guilty enough about accepting money for haying."

"Why should you? Like Grandpa says, he'd have to pay David Boudreau. Why shouldn't he pay you. Fair's fair."

"You don't get paid."

"I'm only twelve. Besides, he's my grandpa."

At that moment, for some inexplicable reason, Nellie broke into a trot as she rounded the corner and headed down the farm lane towards the Chiasson's. Anne pressed against me for a second and kissed me on the cheek. I thought of nothing else until we reached the house and Anne stepped onto the ground.

"Thanks for the ride," called Anne merrily as I circled to go back home. "Don't forget your cows."

Nellie, anxious to be home, began her famous shuffle-trot once more.

That evening I lay in bed on the edge of sleep, but my mind refused to shut down. Anne wanted to be a teacher. I couldn't understand that. A teacher. School for me was a place I looked forward to getting away from, not staying. I wondered if Anne had ever fallen asleep in class. It didn't seem likely. She probably got straight A's. I could feel the hard desk seat pressing against my back. Mr. Smyth's voice echoed close to me, "And this is sleeping beauty." I awoke confused. Another man was standing beside Mr. Smyth. I didn't recognize him.

"Clive, I'd like you to meet Mr. Jameson. Mr. Jameson is visiting our school from the United States."

"Hello, sir," I managed to breathe. Every kid in the class was staring at us.

"Did you doze off, Clive?" said Mr. Jameson.

"Just for a moment, sir."

"What's the problem?" asked Mr. Jameson kindly. I felt beads of sweat break out along my upper lip.

"Nothing."

"Don't you like math?" pursued Mr. Jameson firmly. You could hear the clock ticking in the room.

"I'm not sure I see the point," I said slowly.

"But you see the point of throwing a football," said Mr. Smyth dryly. "Clive provides us with comic relief and some credibility on the lower end of the Bell curve." Mr. Jameson smiled. The class giggled. I could feel myself wincing even now, two months after.

I looked across at Anne and Grandpa wearily unhitching the horses at the end of another day. I was too bone tired to move. My arms hung from my shoulders by habit rather than any firm attachment. This day had clearly started a week ago; this morning, the usual breakfast had been an illusion. God had just put it there to fool me into working past the supper hour once more. Anne was saying something and I could hear her voice. "Don't move," my body replied. "It's another trick to make you work. Move your back off this wagon and I will cause you severe pain—everywhere." I listened to my body. My body knew what it was talking about. I kept my eyes fixed on the rafters, my back immobile. The hay wasn't quite to the rafters yet, but another hundred years and there would be hay enough to see the cattle through the winter. Two different worlds, country and city. It felt like I had been in the country world for a very long time, which suited me fine. Didn't care if I ever saw a bus or a city again.

"Clive, get up." Anne's voice.

"I can't." My voice.

"Why not?" Anne's voice.

"I'm stuck." My voice.

"What's the matter?" Grandpa's voice.

"The wagon's stuck on my back."

"That's serious." Anne's voice.

"There's only one sure cure." Grandpa's voice.

"Oh? What's that?" My voice, a bit suspicious.

"The business end of a pitchfork placed *comme ça*."

"Ouch!" I sat up briskly.

"Works well," said Anne.

"Certainly does," said Grandpa, moving the prongs of the fork once more in my direction.

"I'm cured. Cured! See no hands. I'm standing up. Tell me, Grandpa, what are those?" I asked, pointing towards some poles balanced among the rafters.

"He's trying to change the subject," said Anne warningly.

"No, I'm not. While I was lying on the wagon I noticed those poles. They look like they are for something. See, they have some kind of triangular attachment." Grandpa shaded his eyes to get a better view.

"Oh, those. They're stilts. I made them for the kids many years ago. I'd forgotten they were there."

"For my father?"

"He was a kid once," smiled Grandfather.

"Could he walk on stilts?" I asked.

"Walk? They used to run."

"On stilts?"

"Games of tag and what-not."

"Gosh, could we bring them down? I'd like to try."

"I thought you were too tired to move."

"I am . . . on my feet. Stilts are another matter."

"It's almost supper time," said Anne. "Let's get them some other time."

"Can you walk on stilts, Anne?"

"Sure."

"I'm going to get them. Hold on. It'll only take a minute."

I stepped off the wagon and scampered up the ladder. From the top of the ladder I used the pegs to reach the rafters. I handed the stilts down to Anne. She caught them expertly and stacked them neatly in a corner.

"Come on, show me how to use them," I called.

"No," said Anne stubbornly. "I'm going for supper. I'm starved. After supper." And off she went, leaving me with my collection of stilts. I noticed Grandpa quietly selecting two.

"Try a short one first."

"What do you mean a short one? They all look about the same."

"One with the pegs close to the ground. This pair will do. You rest the top end behind your shoulder blades. Put your hands in front. Hop on and start walking. What d'you know? I can still do it," said Grandpa as he stomped merrily around the barn floor.

"Can I try now?"

"Sure."

"That's it. Top end behind the shoulder, hands in front. One foot on, now the other." It felt strange but I kept my balance. Took one step and then felt the stilts coming apart. The next thing I knew I was sprawled on the ground.

"Have to keep the shaft tucked behind your knee," said Grandpa mildly and proceeded to walk towards the house.

"Grandpa, Grandpa. Wait for me." I ran after him. "Can Anne really walk on stilts?"

"Imagine so."

"Where did she learn?"

"Same place you're learning." Grandpa pushed the kitchen door open and the wonderful aroma of dinner chased all other thoughts from my head. I unlaced my boots, washed up quickly and sat myself down at the table.

"How did it go?" Anne said. I shrugged, my eyes on the piles of fresh baked scones and my nose occupied with the steaming lobster chowder. Grandfather said grace and the evening meal began in silence.

The rain clouds came over the mountains in a dark, swishing mass. Anne looked up at the sky and grinned, the tip of her nose peeling from too much sun. I smiled back also. We had won. The fields stretched down to the barn, clean, flat and green. A half load to go and the hay season would be complete. On the other side of the field Grandfather leaned against the fence and chatted with Arther LeBlanc. "Let the rain come," he seemed to be saying.

"Right now it doesn't seem such a foolish thought to be a farmer," I said.

"We'd better get this final load back to the barn," said Anne, ever practical. "No point in wasting it." Large raindrops began to spatter us. Grandfather turned and walked slowly towards us as we forked the last of the hay into the wagon. He didn't hurry.

"Go ahead, you two," he called. "I'll walk."

"O.K." I cracked the reins and with a jerk Donald and Bill moved off. The horses also seemed to sense we were at the end, and I had to keep them tightly reined to prevent them from trotting. We rolled mightily across the grass towards the barn like a conquering army. We had won! A large warm raindrop caught me in the face. It felt fine.

"Clive?" said Anne.

"Yes."

"Let's do something to celebrate."

"Like what?"

"Go to a movie in Chéticamp."

"How could we get there?" I asked. "It's too far."

"We'd have to get someone to drive us." We drove on in silence, the rain spitting in short fits.

"I wonder why your grandfather wanted to walk?" I looked back at his small figure growing even smaller by the distance and the threatening sky.

"I don't know."

"Maybe you should have walked too," said Anne. "What's the matter?"

"Nothing."

"You're a funny kid, you know that, Clive?"

"A million laughs."

"I don't mean that. I mean you're funny. You talk all the time and you have crazy ideas."

"Like what?"

"Like wanting to quit school and become a tree. That's crazy."

"Why? Some of my best friends are trees."

"So are mine but I don't want to become one."

"So I don't want to be a teacher. So what? Look at the advantages. As a kid I'm a failure. I got kicked off the football team for talking back to the coach. I failed my whole year. As a tree I'd be great. I wouldn't talk. There would be plenty of positions to fill. A good secure future. People would like me. It would be fine."

"People do like you. I like you."

"And you're leaving, right? Back to the store. Back to school."

"So are you," said Anne quietly.

"Ah-ha. That's where you're wrong! Trees don't go to school and they don't move easily!"

"You're crazy, you know that!" said Anne, emphatically but smiling. The wagon bumped into the mow floor and we jumped out to begin unloading the last of the hay. Some time later Grandpa arrived unnoticed.

"Hello. Why the silence? We made it, thanks to you two. You should be proud. Leave that for the moment. I've got something to show you!" We followed Grandfather which was difficult because he was inclined to break into a square-dancing jig and head off in various directions simultaneously. Past the carriage house, the garden, the pig sty, around to the night pasture. "Look, Clive. Nellie's had her foal," cried Anne. And sure enough, there he was. A little spindly-legged creature. A ragamuffin if there ever was one, with a white blaze on his face and three white stockings.

"Bit earlier than I expected," said Grandfather happily, "but beautiful all the same."

"Is he O.K.?" I asked.

"Far as I can tell. The old girl's a bit nippy, but he's moving quite well and feeding!"

"Shouldn't we do something?" I said.

"Like what?" asked Grandfather.

"Wrap him in a blanket?"

"He needs the fresh air and his mother's tongue to dry him off. Tonight Nellie will bed him down in the summer box stall. Everything is just fine."

"Look, she knocked him over." The little fellow struggled, first his hind feet, then his front feet and soon was on all four legs once more. Nellie continued to lick her shaky foal but a little less vigorously.

"Can we go down and pet him?" asked Anne.

"Tomorrow," said Grandfather. "Give him a chance to find his legs."

"When did you find out, Grandpa?"

"Pardon?"

"That the colt was born?"

"At noon. I was just coming up to the house for lunch and on the way decided to check on the mare. And there he was."

"Just being born?" asked Anne.

"Just being born," smiled Grandpa.

"Why didn't you tell us?"

"I thought we'd give the old girl a few hours alone with the little one."

The little fellow's head swung around at the sound of our voices. He was so small standing next to his mother. "What do you want to call him?" asked Grandpa. I regarded the little colt's racey lines. Obviously he would be speedy and strong.

"How about 'Blaze' or 'Buckskin'? His skin is the colour of buckskin." Grandpa smiled.

"It'll get darker," said Grandpa. "That's just his birth colour. What's your vote for a name, Anne?"

"I kind of like Blaze," said Anne.

"It has a nice ring to it," said Grandpa, "but I think we'll call him Donald."

"Donald!" I chewed this pedestrian name over in my mind. It was entirely unsuitable. Besides, we already had a Donald. I pointed this out to Grandfather, to which he replied that perhaps it should be "Young Donald."

"Young Donald." I turned the name over on my tongue. It did have a pleasant ring to it. But I didn't want to give up on Blaze just yet. "The white mark on his face won't go away, will it Grandpa?"

"No, he's got that for life, as well as the stockings. He's going to be handsome. No doubt about that."

"Then why not call him Blaze?"

"Wouldn't you feel foolish pulling a mowing machine in August with a name like Blaze?" countered Grandfather with a grin.

"You've got a point there," I conceded reluctantly. And so Young Donald it was. We stayed and watched for a while longer, the summer afternoon warm and perfect.

Chéticamp Island

Grandpa stirred the porridge sleepily. The bacon made a merry crackling sound. Six o'clock and the sun had already begun brightening the window panes. Another August day had begun. A vague depression settled over my stiff frame. All our worries about rain had been in vain. I poured myself some tea.

"Clive?" asked Grandpa as he ladled out some porridge into my bowl.

"Yes?"

"Do you feel like working today?"

"Not much."

"Well that makes two of us. Why don't we take the day off?"

"Sounds great. What will we do? I think sleep is a good idea," I said, trying unsuccessfully to stifle a yawn.

"Yes," said Grandpa accommodatingly, "but I had something a little more active in mind."

"Oh," I said warily. "Like what?"

"Well, we had that cloudburst yesterday and that means there will be mushrooms out on Chéticamp Island."

"Mushrooms," I said dubiously.

"And it's getting on for blueberry time. I suspect we'll also find some blueberries." Grandpa's eyes fairly sparkled with the thought of blueberries. Mine remained blank. Blueberries conjured no visions of gastronomic delight in my head. Grandpa began to get desperate.

"Clams. We could dig for clams." Clams. Now there was a thought. Clam chowder certainly was tasty.

"O.K.," I said cautiously. "Will we get a ride?" Chéticamp Island was a long way down the road.

"I thought we'd make an outing of it. Take a lunch and go for the day." I nodded absentmindedly. "Do you think we should ask Anne if she wants to come along?" asked Grandfather innocently. "It might make the trip more interesting for you." I sat up with a jerk.

"She's working. She went back to the Co-op today."

"Are you sure? That sounds a bit tough. Why don't you phone and check?"

"No."

"My, my. You're in fine shape this morning." smiled Grandpa. "Maybe you'd better go back to bed until you can find the right side to get up on."

"Sorry," I said. But we finished breakfast in silence. How could I phone Anne? What would I say? My tongue would get tied in knots around clams and outings and the picture I had in my head of her at the other end of the phone. And besides, she had said she was going back to work today. I could see why they wanted Anne back. She was so bright and easy to talk to. No, I might as well admit it to myself. It wasn't the end of haying I was missing. It was Anne.

"You coming, Grandson?"

"Yes. I'll be right there."

"Sure you can stand my company for the whole day," Grandpa grinned. I tossed the lunches at him.

"Stop teasing me."

"I'll stop teasing," he said, suddenly accommodating. "Buckets, don't forget the buckets." I passed them up. "Wallets, lunches, buckets, shovels, assorted containers, one old man and one young man. That's it?"

"That's it," I said smiling. Grandpa clicked the reins and off we went. Bill wasted no time. I wondered if he was even conscious of the weight of the buggy after slaving for so many days in front of the heavy machinery.

"When do we have to take Bill back to Uncle Gerard?" I asked.

"Never."

"Pardon?"

"Gerard has asked me to sell him. Doesn't need him with all his machinery."

"I guess he could get a better price for him while he's behaving."

"Yes, but I sure hate to lose him," said Grandpa finally. "My two old horses together couldn't keep up to this young fellow."

"Why don't you keep him?"

"And have three horses, one foal and eight cows?" Grandpa laughed. "I've already got more horses than I should have." I shook my head. What a pity. Bill was such a beautiful horse.

"We could always sell the old ones," I said reflectively.

"I'll not sell Nellie and Donald," said Grandfather firmly. "They'll stay. They've earned it."

"And Young Donald can take over in a few years," I said as Grandpa veered the buggy towards the Co-op. "Why are we going to the store?" I demanded, seized by a sudden nameless panic.

"I thought we'd pick up some plastic bags."

"Plastic bags! What do we need plastic bags for?"

"Germaine needs them," said Grandpa. "Coming in?"

"No, I'll wait here."

"Suit yourself," said Grandpa equably and disappeared in the direction of the store. I remained alone in the buggy, feeling kind of foolish. Trouble was I just didn't want to see Anne, or, more exactly, I didn't want her to see me. So I sat in the buggy and stared at the horse's rump and felt like one myself.

"Clive." I turned to see Anne coming down the steps of

the store, holding her skirt against her knees. Gone were her dungarees, T-shirt and old straw hat. She looked as she did when I first met her—older, composed and forbiddingly pretty. Only her tanned face gave her recent occupation away. I squeezed down into my jacket and into the seat and into the earth until it closed above me, leaving only a small iron grill through which I could see the sky. It was blue. "Clive." Anne's face appeared above the grill, her face framed by brown curls. "Clive, you're being very rude."

"Why?"

"Because you're supposed to sit up and look at people when they talk to you, that's why."

"I'd like to sit up and talk to you, but I can't."

"I see." Anne's face disappeared from the grill and the sound of her feet against the gravel followed. She was going back to the store. I sat up.

"Anne! Come back."

"What happened?" she asked, returning.

"They let me out for bad behaviour."

"I wish they'd let me out," said Anne, making a face.

"Don't you like working at the Co-op?"

"It's not bad," she said. "I need the money."

"But?"

"But I'd rather be doing something else."

"Like what?" I asked curiously.

"I don't know. What are you and your grandfather doing today?"

"Nothing much."

"You're in a bloody-minded mood today, aren't you?"

"We're going to Chéticamp Island to dig for clams," I blurted out a bit desperately.

"That's great," said Anne, her face lighting up. "I wish I could go."

"It is? You do!" I exclaimed, astonished.

"Sure. Digging for clams is great fun."

"Why don't you come along then? Ask Calèxte."

"It's impossible. We're busy today. In fact, I'd better get back. Why don't you come up to the house tonight and tell me about it?"

"O.K.," I called at Anne's retreating figure. I waited, once more, an inexplicable feeling of lightness surrounding me until Grandfather emerged from the store.

"Sorry I took so long, Clive."

"Oh, that's O.K."

"It is?" exclaimed Grandpa mockingly. "I thought the world was coming to an end."

"The world's just fine, Grandpa! Let's go get those clams!"

"*D'accord, mon petit fils.*" And away we went, Bill's hooves hammering out a staccato rhythm against the pavement. A big station wagon passed us crammed with camping gear and children. As always, the parents seemed to be wedged somewhere between the steering wheel and the bottom of the dashboard. Mom always smiled and waved. The kids always screamed out the side window at us. And Grandfather always touched the peak of his cap politely as the station wagon rolled and belched by like a dispeptic whale on rubber wheels while the camera shuttered. I always sat very straight next to my Grandpa. I was very proud.

After about three-quarters of an hour, we reached the turnoff for Chéticamp Island, and a few minutes later pulled across the mud flats that separated the island from Cape Breton. As we reached the other side, a great blue heron rose from the bullrushes. The wings of the magnificent bird unfolded and extended like sails, slowly, gracefully, taking the bird upwards. The Percheron stopped of his own accord and we waited until the slow, sailing climb of the heron was joined by that of its mate. They circled above us and then headed off down the coast line, their wing beats fading against the sky.

"Let's get the clams on the way back," said Grandpa, breaking the spell with practical manners. "The tide will be lower then, or should be."

"O.K."

We headed up the road that curved towards the top of the island. From the top we could see the village of Chéticamp, spread along the harbourfront, a jumble of colours and intersecting lines: the church, more like a cathedral, cast in the centre of the cluttered scene like a peculiar man-made rock. To the east, north and south the sea swept before us, immense and powerful. The island itself was rugged, rolling countryside dominated by a lighthouse at the farthest end. Sheep and cattle grazed unconcernedly.

"Do all these cattle belong to one farmer?" I asked Grandfather.

"No. The island is a community pasture. Anyone who wants can bring his animals for the season. I used to keep a few young cattle here myself. It's a long drive but once you get them here, you don't have to worry for six months."

"How did you tell which ones were yours at the end of the summer?"

"I used to put bells on my cattle. Each bell had my initials on it."

"Don't see any bells on these animals," I said.

"They use a tattoo now on the inside of the lip or a clip on the ear just like we do at home."

"How do you get close enough to check the clip?"

"A corral is rigged up for a day, usually over there," said Grandpa pointing. "The cattle are rounded up and then each farmer takes a turn picking his animals out. It's a wild day."

"What about the sheep?"

"They're usually left for another month."

"How come?"

"They're tougher and they can find feed where the cattle can't. You don't start the sheep until later either."

"Why is that?"

"Ruin the pasture. They bite it down so low the grass can't get started and the cattle starve. You have to be damn careful when you mix sheep and cattle. It isn't easy running a community pasture. That's why I mostly stayed clear of it."

"I don't understand," I said.

"Well every farmer has his own idea about what is the right mix of cattle to sheep and his own idea about how many animals he should be allowed to run. The sheep men tend to think heavy on the sheep, and the cattle men heavy on the cattle. God! I've seen some real ring-down battles over this place."

"You mean fighting?"

"No. Mostly it was just a lot of arguing. Men yelling at each other like children but there were some fights," said Grandpa with a mischievous smile.

"Tell me more," I said, anxious to hear the gory details.

"Well, in the forties sheep were bringing a pretty good dollar and a lot of the fishermen were beginning to run them on any spare bit of pasture they could find. The island pasture was getting cut up and run down because a lot of men had more sheep than they had pasture for. Simon Aucoin had gone from having about six animals to about thirty in about five years. Simon was a fisherman. He was a huge man, well over six feet, a gaunt fellow with a great, black beard. He used to live up above Chéticamp. A good man, but he had a violent temper. Simon would start a fight as soon as look at you. Well just before the war, arguments were so bad over when and how many sheep should be allowed on the island that if Simon and his neighbour, Jean-Louis Martineau—who had cattle as well as sheep—met on the road, they would stop their horses, jump down from their wagons and start fighting."

"That sounds crazy," I said.

"I suppose it was," replied Grandpa with a smile.

"Didn't they hurt each other?"

"Well they certainly did the time I saw them fight, but that was their last fight. It happened right over there in that clump of woods. It was in the fall. We had come to take the cattle off. The animals had been rounded up and we were just sitting around jawing and waiting for Jean-Louis and a couple of others to arrive. Jean-Louis and his son came over the hill, driving a big team of pure black Percherons. Jean-Louis didn't know one end of a boat from the other but was a good farmer and a good man with horses. *Et mon dieu!* Didn't one of them drop dead right in his tracks."

"One of his horses?"

"That's right. A great big, powerful fellow. He must have weighed more than a ton. Dead as a doornail. Heart attack, I guess. Well we walked over and helped Jean-Louis get the harness off the horse, which wasn't easy, let me tell you, since the other horse was jumping around jerking the dead one. We couldn't cut him free because the harness was too valuable. Finally I got a blindfold over the horse's head. Jean-Louis never said a word. He just borrowed a sled and trussed his horse up on it, ready for the mink farm. We had just finished the dirty work when who should come tripping up the road but Simon Aucoin riding in his ramshackle buckboard, a skinny little horse pulling him along spritely as you please. He pulls up alongside us, looks at the dead horse and smiles as if to say, 'Jean-Louis, you had it coming.' Well I guess Simon knew what was going to happen because Jean-Louis snapped like a branch in a storm. With a cry of rage he launched himself at Simon. Simon jumped down from the buckboard, met him with fists up and the two began to beat at each other with frightful blows. It wasn't a pretty sight. There were children around, Jean-Louis' own son included."

"So what happened?"

"We separated them by force but it didn't do much good. It was clear they would start again the second we released them. Simon was screaming, 'I want to finish this once and for all! Let me at the bastard!' and Jean-Louis was just as complimentary. We didn't have much choice. We let them go on the condition that they finish it off in the woods. They agreed and we let them go. By gosh they looked foolish. Two grown men walking off to beat each other senseless. But it worked."

"What worked?"

"It was their last fight. They never fought again."

"Who won?"

"You'd have to ask the doctors in Chéticamp who fixed them up because neither of them ever admitted to winning or losing. By all accounts, they certainly were a mess. Broken jaw, broken collar bone, teeth missing, bloody eyes."

"Are they still alive?"

"Yes, they are. Simon will be eighty-eight this fall and Jean-Louis must be eighty-six."

"Are they friends?"

"I guess so," said Grandpa smiling. "At least as friendly as they can be. Let's stop here."

"Looks all the same to me," I said.

"Can't you see the blueberries?" asked Grandfather.

"Not a thing," I said, looking down at the hummocky pasture.

"Well I'll show you," said Grandpa jumping down. "Bring the buckets." I followed him to a rocky outcropping over which a small mossy-looking bush was growing.

"See?" he said, pushing the bush to one side so that the blueberries underneath were exposed. Without bothering to pick individual berries, Grandpa raked off a handful and began to fill his bucket. The size of the berries was amazing. I had only seen the supermarket variety—expensive, tiny, seedy things, packed tightly in little cardboard boxes. They did not look very appetizing, but I tried one anyway. The flavour was peculiar, but not bitter or seedy. I tried another and another. Not bad. A little cream and sugar and they'd be all right. I had thought it ridiculous that Grandfather had chosen buckets to carry the berries we picked, but now it seemed possible. I raked the leaves, catching the ripe berries in the palm of my hand. One for me, one for the bucket. My bucket was definitely not filling very fast. I sat down and began to harvest the berries in earnest. Handful after handful spilled into the bucket.

The work was hypnotizing and very peaceful. Grandpa had a saying that a hard-working man never realized the work was hard until he was through. I looked down at my hands that had become rough and calloused from working with a pitchfork. Haying had been hard work. Yet I would start all over again if I had the chance. I leaned back. The blueberry bushes made a mighty fine bed from which to watch the sky. I tried to imagine the black spaces beyond the light blue of our own horizons. Who said that the universe is not only more complicated than you think, it's more complicated than you can think? Was it Albert Einstein or Albert Schweitzer? I always got the two of them mixed up. From my angle on the sky the universe didn't seem that complicated. You had the earth, on which we were presently pleasantly rotating, the sky above us, the sea around us and that was the last thing I remembered.

"Clive?" Grandpa's voice.

"I'll be right down, Grandpa." My voice.

"Down? Down where?" Grandpa's voice.

I opened my eyes and instead of the bedroom ceiling I saw the sky over Chéticamp Island.

"Sorry," I said automatically.

"Sure you don't want to sleep a little longer?" grinned Grandfather.

"Oh," I groaned, my back protesting as I sat up. "How long have I been asleep?"

"By the look of the berries in your bucket, I'd say a good long while."

"Feels like days. Where's Bill?" I asked.

"I set him free to get a little lunch."

"I could do with some lunch myself," I said.

"That's why I woke you. I've got the sandwiches. Let's go."

"Where we going?"

"I thought we'd go over and see Ti-Jean."

"Who's he?"

"Ti-Jean Gallant is the man who keeps the lighthouse," said Grandpa and we set off towards the far end of the island. As we approached the point on which the lighthouse was located, I noticed the roar of the sea increased until it drowned the sound of the shore birds and our own passage. There were three small white painted houses with green trim located in a line beside the lighthouse.

"Grandpa?"

"Yes, Clive."

"How come there are three houses?"

"Because there are three lighthouse keepers."

"Why? I always thought there was only one to a lighthouse." Grandpa smiled.

"A lighthouse keeper needs time off like anyone else. There's Ti-Jean." A huge man lumbered out of a small door at the base of the lighthouse.

"He doesn't look very small to me," I said under my breath, regarding the man's bear-like figure.

"Allo, William!" the lighthouse keeper called, his voice booming along on the sound of the surf.

"Good day to you, Ti-Jean. I've brought you a visitor, my grandson, Clive."

"*A Fernand?*" asked Monsieur Gallant.

"*C'est ça,*" confirmed Grandfather.

"*Bonjour, mon Clive. Ça va?*"

"*Très bien, monsieur,*" I replied.

"So you've still got a job," said Grandpa, smiling.

"Still got a job," said Ti-Jean gravely. "But not for long."

"Bah! That's what you've been saying for years," said Grandpa. "The government has got to keep men at the lighthouse."

"Why's that?" I asked innocently.

"So that there's someone to show boys like you around," said Ti-Jean with a smile. "Would you like to go up and take a look?"

"That would be great."

"Let's go then," said Ti-Jean. "You up for it, William? I've got something to show you, too."

"I'll make it," said Grandpa. "Perhaps a little slower, but I'll make it." Ti-Jean entered the lighthouse and we followed. What a climb it was. The big man seemed to float effortlessly above us as we circled and circled upwards inside the tower. Grandpa began to stop on each landing, contemplating the next assent. Gradually the turns got sharper until we emerged in the room at the top. A huge machine that didn't look like a light at all dominated the centre of the room. Down below, we could see the ocean break silently against the cliff. It was so far down my head swam. I shut my eyes and stepped back from the edge.

Grandpa and Ti-Jean were examining a bank of machinery. "Didn't I tell you, William?" said Ti-Jean. "Here it is. See, the electric light is self-cleaned and automatically changed when it's burned out. The spare lamp is brought into focus and lit *comme ça.* Neat, eh?"

"Who turns it on?" asked Grandfather, sounding dubious.

"The light's controlled by a sun valve. Electricity for the light, the fog signal and the radio beacon is powered at the lighthouse by four main generators and there's a standby diesel set. They start up and shut down automatically according to the sun valve."

"It's hard to believe," said Grandpa. "What if this blessed sun valve doesn't work?"

"That's what this machine is for. They're building a control station. I'm not sure where, maybe in Halifax. If something goes wrong, it'll be recorded and sent out immediately."

"Then what do they do?" asked Grandpa scornfully. "Send a mechanic out by plane in the middle of a sou-east?" Ti-Jean shrugged.

"Makes no difference what you or I say, William. It's what the government wants and the government doesn't want lighthouse keepers anymore. Too expensive. Cheaper to do it this way, I guess."

"What happens to you, Jean?" asked Grandfather.

"We stay here for another year until the bugs are out of this machinery. Then we'll be shifted someplace else."

"So you're not going to lose your government job," smiled Grandfather broadly.

"Like I've said all along, William, they're just phasing us out slowly. I'll probably replace some fellow that's been pensioned off down the coast. Besides, I don't have that long to go myself. Bah. Not worth thinking about. Let's go down for lunch."

We began the descent from the lighthouse to the small house and Mrs. Gallant's kitchen.

"That's the last time I'll climb your wretched tower before they turn me under," said Grandfather with a grimace to Ti-Jean. "My old legs are still trembling."

"Have another cup of tea, William," said Mrs. Gallant.

"Well, there's one thing for sure," smiled Ti-Jean. "I won't be climbing any lighthouses when I'm your age, William. They'll all be automatic. By God, Catherine," he said to his wife. "Remember Scatari Island? The stairs in that tower were something else!"

"I'm glad we're not there any more," said Madame Gallant firmly. "It was so isolated."

"Did you see any shipwrecks?" I asked, curious.

"Never," said Ti-Jean dryly.

"Don't tease the boy," said Madame spritely. "Tell him about a shipwreck."

"What's there to tell?" said Ti-Jean defensively. "They're all the same."

"You've seen more than one?" I asked, astonished.

"Yes."

"What happens?"

"It starts with one of two things. Either the captain loses his bearings in the storm and the boat ends up on the rocks. Or his engine isn't strong enough, and the boat gets blown up on the rocks. The second used to be quite common, but nowadays it's quite rare. Once the boat is on the rocks, it's finished. The waves just pound the ship against the cliffs until she either breaks in half and sinks, or turns over and sinks. It's not very complicated."

And with that Ti-Jean ended the conversation on shipwrecks. He seemed angry. I wasn't sure whether he was angry at me or ships, so I just nodded and kept to myself until we left.

"You're quiet, Clive," said Grandpa as we walked back towards the buggy. "What are you thinking?"

"Nothing."

"Nothing, is it? Well, while you're thinking of nothing,

will you come over here and help me fill this bucket with mushrooms?"

"Are you sure they aren't poisonous?"

"Well, I don't know if they are *champignons de Paris* or not, but I do know they taste mighty fine in clam chowder."

"O.K." We began to pick the leafy-looking mushrooms. It was a good deal simpler than picking blueberries. In a remarkably short time, the bucket was filled to overflowing.

"Will Aunt Germaine use all these?" I asked doubtfully.

"Probably not."

"Let's give some to the LeBlancs on our way home then."

"Good idea," said Grandpa. He pulled out his pocket watch to inspect it. "Time we were going or the tide will catch us. Can you get Bill while I clean up here?"

"Sure." I went over to the buggy and took out a small canister of oats we had brought for the occasion. He was nowhere to be seen. I went over the hill calling his name and banging the can. There he was, silhouetted against the horizon. I called his name and Bill moved away from me, intent on grazing rather than pulling us home. I banged the can once more. His ears pricked up. It never failed. He started to move towards me and then began to trot, anxious to get his teeth settled into the oats. I always felt a rush of excitement as the giant horse slowed calmly at the sound of my voice. I let him eat for a moment or two and then quietly led him over to the buggy. Poor Bill, betrayed by his stomach once more.

"Ready?" said Grandpa as he packed away the last of the blueberries in an odd assortment of bottles.

"Ready," I said and we began to bounce over the field towards the road. Once we hit the road, Bill really started to fly and to my great delight, in a spray of gravel and thunder of hooves, we whirled past a meandering car-load of tourists. When we hit the tide flats, the tide had already begun to turn. Grandpa wasted no time. We parked Bill, then with shovel and bucket in hand I followed Grandpa, who was already turning up clams. "Grandpa, are they ever big!" I called, holding up a large shell.

"Fair size. Better get some water in your bucket."

"This much?"

"A little less. Just enough to keep them cool on the way home. That's it."

"Grandpa?"

"Yes, Clive."

"Was Ti-Jean angry at me?"

"No."

"He sure sounded like it."

"I know, but it was the idea of the shipwreck that was bothering him, not you."

"What shipwreck?"

"Well it was a while ago—a long liner was coming into the harbour during a big storm. Ti-Jean was the light-house keeper. The light failed. Ti-Jean fixed it and when he looked up from his work, the long liner which had been labouring towards the harbour mouth was smashed up against the foot of the cliffs, about a hundred yards from the lighthouse. The men were clinging to the ship but the waves pushed them overboard into the water. Ti-Jean and the two other keepers tried to get lines to them. They got one man up the cliff but the two others drowned almost at their feet. I think Ti-Jean blames himself."

"Was it his fault?"

"They had an investigation."

"What did it say?"

"Said it wasn't Ti-Jean's fault."

"Then why does he blame himself?"

"I don't know."

"Did they figure out what went wrong?"

"No. The captain drowned and the fellow who was saved wasn't sure what had happened either. He was getting packed up to go home when suddenly the ship heeled around from the harbour mouth and began to be pushed broadside by the storm along the coast towards the point."

"What do you think happened?"

"Just one of those things," Grandpa shrugged. "Maybe he lost power for a moment. Maybe the wind caught the boat just right . . . who knows?"

We continued to dig for clams. There were so many of them. It was as if someone had put them here in long even rows for us. I wondered where they all came from but I decided not to ask Grandpa. He was about questioned out for today. I straightened up and noticed another couple of figures further on down the beach turning the muddy sand for clams. The late afternoon sun sent a million sparkling lights alive and dancing across the surface of the water. It was difficult to believe this tranquil scene could be other than benign.

Blue Hanover

Bill regarded with suspicion the ramp leading up to the truck. I talked to him quietly, gently, insisting with my hand on the halter. He didn't budge. Front feet planted firmly, eyes rolling, Bill wasn't going anywhere, least of all into the back of a rickety-looking pick-up. The big horse flattened his ears and curled his lip until large, flat square teeth were exposed. The message was clear. "Don't push me, I'm scared." I wasn't, but I was getting there. Bill was a lot bigger than I was. I looked across for some help but Grandpa was talking to the buyer, a Mr. McGuire, a small, intense man from Cape North. Neither seemed to notice my problem. I didn't want to admit defeat, but there wasn't much choice.

"Grandpa. He doesn't want to go." Grandpa and the buyer strolled over. Grandpa took one side of the halter, McGuire the other. Bill braced himself as if getting ready to exert himself against a superior force. The whites of his eyes showed dangerously. Grandpa signalled McGuire to stop pulling.

"You in a hurry?" asked Grandpa.

"Not especially," said the man. "I thought you said he was gentle?"

"He is," said Grandpa defensively. "He'll do anything you want him to do."

"Except get in the back of my truck."

"Maybe that's because he weighs more than your truck

162

does," said Grandpa with a smile. "You sure you can get him home in it?"

"As long as he stays quiet," said McGuire. "If he starts to twist around, I'll be in trouble. You know what the road home's like, William."

"Then let's not start him off nervous," said Grandpa. "Can you move the truck over into the sun? Clive, go get a bucket of water and his small grain bag."

When I returned, Bill was tethered behind the truck under the full force of the midday sun. He still looked like he wasn't going anywhere. Grandpa took the two buckets and placed them halfway into the truck so that Bill could see them but would not get at them without at least partially entering the truck. The strategy was clear. We retired to the house for lunch and left Bill to ponder the nature of his predicament.

"It's a good thing you're selling him, William," said Mr. McGuire to Grandpa as he polished off his third dessert.

"Why's that?"

"Because you never know when a horse is going to die on you. That's one advantage of a tractor. When it's broke you can always go to the garage. A horse goes six feet under."

"I don't know," said Grandpa mildly. "I've had Donald and Nellie for better than twenty years. They're still going strong. I just got a colt off Nellie, too. Don't see many tractors that can give you a new tractor." McGuire smiled.

"Maybe so, but I had a young horse just like the grey one out there. One day he was the best horse I ever had. The next day he was dead and I was out three hundred and twenty dollars. That could happen to you, William." Grandpa shrugged.

"What happened?" I asked, curious.

"Like I said. He was a young horse. Couldn't tire him out. After I got the harness off him and set him outside for the evening, he'd always lay down and roll and twist on his back like he was taking a bath."

"Donald does that," I said.

"You see, William," said McGuire dourly.

"What's rolling have to do with the horse dying," I persisted.

"Well, a horse's insides are loosely attached. Sometimes they get twisted. If they get twisted badly enough, the horse can't digest its food. My young horse twisted his guts rolling and that was that."

"Did you call the vet?"

"Sure, and he shot him," said McGuire. On that brief note, we finished our tea.

"Well, let's go take a look at Bill," said Grandpa. "Open the door quietly." Sure enough, Bill's front hooves were planted firmly in the truck, his back hooves on the ramp. He was making comfortable sounds as he ate. I squeezed by into the truck and moved the pails to the front. Bill followed like a lamb, betrayed by his stomach once more.

"You sure he's going to be all right, Grandpa?" I asked as we watched the pick-up sway down the lane towards the highway.

"They'll make it."

"No. I mean do you think Mr. McGuire will take care of Bill?"

"Oh, sure," said Grandpa. "He'll work him harder than I would but that's because he's got a bigger farm. McGuire's a good man with horses. You have to be these days."

"What do you mean?"

"In the old days everyone owned horses. If something went wrong, you could always get someone to help. Now you have to rely more on yourself. Look at McGuire. He had to come fifty miles to get a replacement for his horse. And that's an easy distance. If it's harness or machinery, you've got to send away for it."

"I see what you mean," I said. Grandpa reached into his pocket and took out a roll of dollar bills. "Three hundred and twenty dollars," said Grandpa partly to himself. "That's seventy dollars more than Gerard expected. Not bad for an old horsetrader, eh?"

"Do we get to keep the seventy dollars?"

"That's what I understand from Gerard. What shall we do with the money?" asked Grandpa, again as if he was talking more to himself.

"Put it in the bank," I said.

"That's what I always do. Be careful and save." Grandpa flipped the money in his hands. "You know what I'd like to do with this seventy dollars?"

"What?"

"Go to the races tomorrow at Inverness."

"Then let's do it," I said with great sang-froid.

"No, we can't," said Grandfather with a sigh. "Your aunt would have a fit. Besides, we can't really afford it."

"Do we have to spend the whole seventy dollars?" I asked, never having been to the races before.

"Let's see," said Grandpa. "There's five dollars for the taxi fare. Five dollars for lunch. We'd have to bet on a few races. Let's say ten dollars for bets."

"That's twenty."

"Is that all?" said Grandpa seemingly impressed. "I thought it would cost more."

"I'll ask Germaine," I said boldly.

"You will?" asked Grandpa alarmed.

"Leave it to me," I said purposefully.

"No, you don't."

"Will you ask then?"

"No. What are you going to say?" asked Grandfather nervously.

"Give me a second. Let's see. Why don't I suggest we split the seventy dollars? Germaine gets a trip into Cheticamp to do some shopping and visit Uncle Phil, and we go up to Inverness."

"Seems fair enough. . . ." said Grandfather, but he still seemed dubious. He needn't have been. Germaine gave her O.K., though it was followed by a mild lecture on betting, David Boudreau and the like.

As the taxi lurched around the final curve, my eyes strained to catch a glimpse of the racetrack. There it was—or, more precisely, there the stands were. Cars, trucks and trailers parked in regular rows across a large field blocked our view of the racetrack itself. The taxi slowed and stopped at the rutted entrance to the field. Grandpa and I disembarked. The taxi driver yelled for us to keep our shirts and Grandpa smiled and said we would.

"Can you bet your shirt?" I asked as we walked towards the track between the rows of horse trailers and cars.

"In a manner of speaking," said Grandpa. "But it's not advisable. Racing is like beer, it's best taken in small doses."

I grimaced. But before I could reply, a roly-poly man leading a small bay mare burst out from between two parked trucks and almost knocked us over. He abruptly halted his headlong flight, the little mare banging her nose into his back. Grandfather, who was on the inside, was knocked head over heels. The man bent down to give Grandfather a hand up.

"Daniel, you great balloon! Why don't you watch where you're going?"

"William. You old coot. What brings you to the races?"

"The races," said Grandfather with a smile. "How are you Dan?"

"I should be asking you that," said Daniel as Grandfather got to his feet. "But, fine as you look to be," said the roly-poly man, his round apple face curving into sunny creases. "Who's this?" he said looking down over his wide belly towards me.

"My grandson, Clive."

"Well, how do you do," he said extending his hand.
"And a fine, big lad you are too."

"How do you do," I said, and we solemnly shook
hands. The useless ceremony over, for he neglected to
say who he was, the man turned his attention back to
Grandfather.

"Well, William, you coming to the sale after the
races?"

"No," said Grandfather briefly.

"Why not? Get yourself a fast, young thing that can get
your buggy out of first gear. You're tempted, I can see
you're tempted."

"Of course, I am," said Grandpa, a little irritably. "But
you know I can't afford it. How much you selling the bay
for?"

"A steal at nine hundred dollars," laughed the man.

"Got any tips for us, Danny?" asked Grandfather ignoring the price.

"Time Flies in the third. See you later," and the roly-
poly man trundled off, the bay mare still pushing him
from behind.

"Who's that?" I asked.

"Danny Deveau. Horse trader, horse trainer and horse
thief."

"Has he ever stolen a horse?"

"Well, maybe not outright but as close as you can come
without slipping the halter over the horse's head and
leading him out of the stable."

"How did you get to meet him?"

"Danny? I've known him before he knew himself. He's
Gilles son. Gilles Deveau, the man who owns the garage
in the village."

"Oh yes," I said, the friendly grey-haired image of
Gilles Deveau popping up before my eyes. "Strange that
his son ended up with horses instead of cars, isn't it?"

The loudspeakers interrupted Grandpa's intended

reply and we hurried toward the rail to catch the first race. The horses were circling the track. How dainty they were. They looked more like children's ponies than the horses I was used to.

"When do they start, Grandpa?"

"In a minute, and they must line up evenly behind that car with the contraption on the back."

"Programs, programs," called a boy. "Want a program mister?"

"One, please," said Grandfather and handed the boy 25 cents.

He passed the program to me without looking at it, keeping his eyes on the horses. I glanced through the sheets of paper—eight races in all, but most of it didn't make much sense to me, a jumble of numbers and initials. The only name I recognized was Time Flies driven by D. Deveau.

"Grandpa, are we going to bet on Time Flies?" I asked, but just then the loudspeaker blared "They're off!" and the first race was underway. I strained to catch sight of the horses on the other side of the track, but they remained indistinct figures until the horses came pounding around the near corner, their legs going like pistons. I could see why the drivers had goggles and crash helmets. Dirt and dust flew as the drivers jockeyed their horses and the tiny two-wheeled sulkies for position. Three horses were well out in front, the rest packed into a tight bunch a couple of lengths behind the leaders. Then, number two, Warbonnet, started to open up the distance between himself and his two companions. They challenged him on the backstretch but he fought off their surges and coming around the final curve, he was all alone. It turned out Warbonnet was the favourite.

"Are you hungry Clive?"

"Starved."

"Foolish question," said Grandpa. And we made our way towards a small concession by the stands.

"What'll you have?" asked the man behind the counter.

"You go first," said Grandpa.

"Is this lunch?" I asked, a bit uncertain of the time and occasion. Grandpa glanced at his watch.

"This is lunch."

I read the menu which was written in red plastic letters above the counter and made up my mind quickly.

"Three hot dogs, french fries, onion rings, a root beer and some ice cream."

"Forgotten anything?" asked the man dryly.

"No, that's it."

"What'll it be for you William?"

"Salmon sandwich, cole slaw and a beer," said Grandpa.

"Coming up."

I glanced up at the red letters once more. There was no beer written up there. Grandpa didn't read very well. I wondered how I should tell him. He was a bit shy about his ability with letters. I cleared my throat and then whispered.

"Grandpa."

"Yes," he whispered back.

"There's no beer advertised."

"I'm not surprised."

"Why?"

"Fogerty's not allowed to sell it."

"Why not?"

"That's the law."

"Won't we get in trouble if you buy it then?"

"I doubt it."

"How come? There's Mounties around. I've seen them."

"Fogerty's the mayor."

"Of Inverness?"

"Of Inverness," whispered Grandfather.

"I see." I whispered back totally confused.

"Three hot dogs, french fries, onion rings, a root beer and one ice cream," said the mayor of Inverness.

"Thank you," I said.

"Beer, sandwich and cole slaw for you William."

"Thanks. How much?"

"Three-o-five," said Mr. Fogerty.

Grandpa paid him and we made our way to the stands. The second race was about to begin, but to be honest, the prospect of the feast laid out beside me on the wooden bleacher occupied me more than the race did. I peered curiously into the paper cup as Grandpa pulled the lid off. It was beer all right. There was no mistaking the pungent odor. I'd remember it all the days of my life.

"Want a sip?" asked Grandpa blithely.

"No thanks," I shuddered, recalling the appalling sickness the day after my adventure in the well. "Root beer will do me just fine." And I went back to carefully spreading relish and mustard on my hot dogs. It seemed like about a million years since I had last bitten into a genuine hot dog. The taste was heavenly.

"Grandpa?"

"Don't talk with your mouth full."

"Sorry."

"Grandpa?"

"Yes."

"You were telling me how Daniel got involved with horse racing instead of cars like his father."

"I was? Oh, yes. Let's see now. It all began at the fall fair in Margaree Forks. Oh, Daniel couldn't have been any older than you are now—12 or so. He won a standard bred in a raffle contest. They called out the lucky number and Daniel had it. It was that simple."

"Did his parents let him keep it?"

"They didn't want to. In fact, Gilles approached me to sell the horse for him. He wanted Daniel to save the money for a college education, but Daniel made such a fuss, they abandoned the idea. My children never would have been permitted to keep a hay burner. I don't think they would even have thought of it. But Danny was an only child. I guess they could afford it. So Gilles let him keep the horse in a small barn at the back of the garage that was a left-over from when Gilles' father ran a few cows for the house."

"Did Daniel ever race him?"

"No. Mostly, he just trotted him around and felt very proud."

"How long did he keep him?"

"Until he was fourteen or so, then he agreed to sell him. I guess by that time he realized there wasn't much point in keeping a racehorse if you can't get him to a track to race him."

"Were his parents happy then?"

"They were but it didn't last long because a year or so later Daniel ran away."

"He ran away? How old was he then?"

"Just turned fifteen."

"Where did he go?"

"McDonald stables in Sydney. A big outfit."

"Weren't his parents upset?"

"Of course. Daniel wasn't just their only son, he was their only child."

"Did they go and get him?"

"They went down to talk to Daniel but they couldn't persuade him to come home. The McDonalds were nice people and Daniel seemed content, so they left him."

"Quit school and everything?"

"Quit school and everything," repeated Grandfather with a smile.

"And he never went back. Not that quitting school ever worried Daniel. But he sure worried his parents. I don't think Gilles ever quite got over it."

"Why was that?"

"Well, it's my guess Gilles never really wanted Danny to go to college. He wasn't really suited to it—even a blind man could tell that. College was just a diversion. Gilles wanted his son as a partner in the garage."

"Did they send Daniel money?"

"Not a thing. Gilles said if he wanted to live like an adult, he could damn well work like one. That didn't worry Daniel or so he told me—he was going to be a millionaire. And I think I half believed him."

"Why?"

"Well, he had a sense for business and a sense for horses."

"Did he make a million?"

"I'm not sure. He did well, very well, for a while. By the time he was 22 he had a big farm up on the Margaree. A dirt track out back and a stable full of horses. It was a beautiful farm, lots of bottom land on the river. A doctor from Upper Canada owns it now."

"What happened?"

"He lost it to the bank and ever since then he's been up and down. Never too far down, mind you, but never too far up either."

"What level is he at now?"

"He's got a small place—just enough to pasture a few horses."

"He looks prosperous from here," I said as Daniel drove by in the pre-race parade, resplendent in green and gold colours.

"Daniel has always had style. Still does," said Grandpa with a smile.

"Shall we bet on Time Flies?" I asked. "That's his horse."

"Why not?" said Grandpa, his eyes never leaving the

little bay mare. "She looks pretty good from here. What are the odds?"

"3 to 1 I think," I said squinting at the board.

"Shall we bet to win or show?" asked Grandpa.

"Win," I said, automatically. "What's 'place'?"

"Second."

"You can bet on a horse to come in second?" I asked, surprised.

"Or third. Third is called 'to show.' "

"That makes it more complicated."

"It does."

"Let's bet on Time Flies to win," I said resolutely. Grandpa pursed his lips as if expecting news from afar at any moment.

"O.K.," he said finally. "Wait here."

"I'm not going anywhere," I said, my stomach listing 45 degrees to starboard.

"Save some ice cream for me," said Grandpa and he went off in his slight, elfish way to place the bet. The race had already started when Grandpa returned. Time Flies was locked back in the pack running about fifth. Grandpa looked pretty grim.

"What's the matter?"

"Nothing," he said.

We settled down to watch the race. In the backstretch, Time Flies picked up into fourth and on the far turn he moved into third, but there didn't seem much chance the little bay would catch the two leaders. People stood as they came around the final turn. Daniel swept around to the outside taking too much room, but the little mare responded with a brilliant burst of speed and began challenging the two leaders. Whips cracked and all three horses seemed to strain in one even line towards the finish. I couldn't cry out. It was as if the moment was suspended. They seemed to cross the line together in a dead heat, but the board rang up Time Flies as the winner.

"She won! We won!" I cried, jumping up and down like

a maniac. "We're rich. Rich! Fifteen dollars. We won fifteen dollars Grandpa!"

"No we haven't," said Grandpa glumly.

"Why not?"

"Because I changed my mind at the last minute and bet on Time Flies to show."

"Oh no!"

"Oh yes. And to make things worse, everyone knew Time Flies was going to win. I overheard two rail birds on the way back. Apparently, Time Flies is the best animal Daniel's had in years."

"Damn," I said.

"Damn is right," said Grandpa. "I should have known better than to bet I couldn't win on a horse race unless the other horses were running on three legs.

"From now on, I'll content myself with watching." I nodded. That seemed sensible to me as we watched the losing horses leave the track.

"Unless I get another tip," said Grandpa with a wicked grin.

"We've still got five dollars in the betting fund," I said.

"What are you doing?" asked Grandpa in bewilderment.

"Lying down. I can see the track from here as well as sitting up."

Grandpa shook his head. "I've never seen such a boy for sleeping. Every time I turn around you're snoring—in fields, under hay ricks, beside fence posts—I'm surprised you just didn't curl up on top of the milk can at the bottom of the well and just 'take five' until we found you."

"We've been up since six o'clock," I protested mildly. "Besides, I'm not going to fall asleep. I'm just going to watch this race lying down. It's more comfortable."

"Would you like the program over your face so you can study it while you watch?"

"No thanks," I replied, concentrating on the blue sky above. The wooden bleacher felt surprisingly comfortable. I shifted my gaze to the track. In front of the stands, they were taking photos of Daniel and Time Flies. I wondered idly how much money he had won. It must be in the program somewhere. I'd check it later. The root beer, hot dogs, onion rings, french fries and ice cream had combined to form a wonderful sense of well-being that radiated from the centre of my stomach to all other parts of my body. The instructions from headquarters were firm. Stay on your back, Clive. Do not be tempted to move in any way. I stayed on my back. I turned my head to look at the race track. From this perspective, it seemed very pretty, like a painting. But the excitement that had coursed along the rail like electricity seemed to have dissipated in the journey from the track to the bleachers. From here, the racetrack had the mild feeling of a church social. People wandering around lazily in the afternoon sun. The activity on the track didn't appear to be connected to the tranquil comfort of the day's unravelling.

A church social. Germaine would have been shocked at that notion. She had said, "Father, I don't believe you should be taking the boy to see horse races. I'm not sure Fern would approve." And Germaine had clattered and banged dishes for a while as she always did when she was annoyed. "Oh I don't suppose there's any harm in going," she had said finally, "but . . ." The sentence was never completed. I dried the dishes and Grandpa rocked sleepily in his chair. "But," Germaine had said. I wondered what the "but" was. Germaine and Dad were a lot alike, always quick with the yes-buts. Yes, but horse races are not on the ladder to somewhere. The only trouble was they never quite explained where the somewhere was.

Maybe they were afraid I would turn out like Daniel Deveau, and become a tramp lodged between a couple of bales of hay and my favourite harness horse. Didn't seem to have bothered Daniel much. A lot of destinations had "tramp" or "can't" written on them—hockey or football player, sailor. So where was somewhere? Somewhere was good marks at school, going to bed early, being polite and that kind of thing and if you did it for many years—what then? You got an education and a good job. What was a good job? A good job was one where you wore a white shirt and tie, and carried a briefcase. A good job was a lot like school. Trouble was, I didn't like school. So what was the point? Why not run away like Daniel? Why not? Because I had this awful suspicion that there was more to it than just a good job. Nobody had the guts to come out and say it straight out. But it had to do with superiority. You would be wiser. You would see new horizons. That was what you would miss if you missed an education and weren't polite. Grandpa believed it. Father believed it. Germaine believed that you were inferior without an education. Because without an education, you couldn't see those further horizons. And it was all wrong because Grandpa was as smart as anyone I knew and he had trouble with his letters. And Germaine, in her way, knew it was not true also. And so did Dad. But it didn't stop Dad from saying that a doctor can be a farmer, but a farmer can't be a doctor. That was a favourite line of his . . . I wondered how many doctor-farmers we had walking around. (He usually pronounced this piece of wisdom when looking at my report card.) The way Dad talked, the hills were crawling with them—stethoscopes swinging merrily from their necks as they followed behind horse and plow. But I'd never seen one. I just heard about them.

The earth revolved lazily under the sun and I revolved on top of a bleacher fastened to the earth, which was swimming in space. That's what I would be—an explorer, sitting on a bleacher, inside a whale swimming in space.

Except, someone was gnawing sharply at my kneecap, regularly at my kneecap. A whale fly perhaps. I tried to brush it away. But the gnawing persisted. I opened my eyes and saw nothing but bright dancing white flies. Tiny dots circling in the sun. I blinked once more and dots composed themselves into Grandfather, who was striking the edge of the bleacher and part of my knee with his program while yelling *"Allez, Daniel! Allez!"* Apparently the horses were pounding down the stretch. I sat up partly to get a better view of the race and partly to get out of the way of Grandpa's whip hand. The blood rushed to my head, making me dizzy, and I lay back down again to get my balance.

The lead horses crossed the finish line and Grandpa let the program fly from his hand in disgust. It didn't look like we were doing so well.

"Fine help, you were," said Grandpa scathingly, noticing I had revived.

"I didn't do anything," I said, feeling quite groggy.

"That's just the point."

"You said you weren't going to bet any more."

"Well I did."

"How much did we lose?"

"Ten dollars. Ten whole dollars."

"We brought the ten dollars to bet."

"But not to lose," said Grandfather glumly. "I was up at one point. Ah well."

"What race are we at?" I enquired, hoping to take his mind off the problem of the ten dollars.

"That was the last."

"You mean you let me sleep through five races," I said shocked.

"What do you mean 'let'?" roared Grandfather. "I thought you had died!"

I rubbed my eyes sleepily. Grandpa could grump, but the day was young yet.

"Why don't we go and take a look at the horse sale."

"Why?"

"It might be fun. Besides, I've never been to a horse sale before."

"Nothing much to it," said Grandfather still grumbling, but I could see he had perked up already at the thought. "There will be some fine horses at the sale. I wonder if Daniel really will sell that bay mare of his?" Grandpa stood up, stretched and began to descend the bleachers, talking all the while. "The sales are where Daniel really makes his money, not on the racetrack."

"Why is that?"

"If you're lucky, winning at the racetrack will feed your horses and that's about it. Rent, travel, equipment, your own grub—that's all got to be paid out of horse trading, horse training and something else," said Grandfather darkly.

"What do you mean something else?"

"Honest work," said Grandfather grinning, his humour restored. "But as little as possible, if I know Daniel." The ramshackle rail fence which passed for the sales ring was already lined with men. There were three rows of benches behind the rail. Grandfather and I sat on the top one. We didn't wait long. The first horse entered the ring followed by the auctioneer. A heavy-set, ruddy-faced man. He carried a walking cane but handled it more like a weapon. The auctioneer surveyed the assembled farmers with confidence and a practiced eye. When his gaze swung in our direction, I had the peculiar urge to hide and was glad when he switched it elsewhere. With a jolt, I realized the auctioneer was Fogerty the bootlegger. Suddenly, his eyes picked something out in the crowd and he began to hammer out words in a high staccato voice, as if minting each one between hammer and anvil.

The only thing I understood was that the sale had begun. The horse in the ring moved uneasily, his eyes wide and fearful of the crowd and the sound of the auctioneer's voice. The auctioneer's cane traced a line along the back of the horse, his voice mounting in intensity as he did so. "Going once, going twice—sold to Chris Thomas of North Margaree." The horse was quickly led out of the ring by a handler and another brought in. The same rhythm repeated itself. A handler led the horse a couple of times around the ring, then the horse was allowed to walk freely while the buyers examined his actions. The bidding would start and I began to get a feel for the sounds the auctioneer made. The words weren't important. It was the ebb and flow of the chant that counted. A musical exhortation to buy that rose and fell and flowed out to the audience and back to the ring again, the sound of the auctioneer's voice rippling like a stream. Fogerty's head would move ever so slightly at the sight of a new offer. His bright, restless eyes lighting up for a moment, the chant breaking clearly around the sound of a hard number, 670-675, before returning to the staccato stream. It was exciting.

The prices the horses were selling were downright scary—700, 800, 1200 dollars. I wondered where all the money was coming from? There couldn't have been more than 40 or 50 men in the audience, most in common working clothes. Yet, bucketfuls of money were moving briskly between sellers and buyers. The horses changed hands quickly. Grandpa poked me with his elbow and my eyes returned to the ring. It was Daniel's little bay mare, Time Flies. She stepped into the ring daintily, her ears cocked, her coat glistening. Time Flies was a winner. It was written all over her. There was a heightened interest among the assembled men.

The bidding began slowly at what seemed like a high price—nine hundred dollars—nevertheless the price spiraled steadily upwards. It soon became clear the contest was between two men. A large, prosperous-looking man in a white shirt and grey flannels and a young fellow dressed entirely in denim. The bidding see-sawed. Each man being cautious, but determined. "Going once, going twice at eighteen-hundred-and-fifty dollars," but before Fogerty could say "sold," the young man in demin put in another bid. And the price went up again. Around the ring all was silent. No shuffling. No muttering. Two thousand. Then two thousand-two hundred, two thousand-five hundred, three thousand. Three . . . three thousand, going once, going twice—sold to the young man in the denim jacket. The young man smiled a bit weakly, but he smiled. The large man in the white shirt shrugged as if to say there are other horses, but his shrug was unconvincing. Time Flies was clearly the sale prize. She had sold for twelve-hundred dollars more than the nearest competitor. After her sale, the buyers seemed wary of high prices, and determinedly kept their bids low.

"Grandpa."

"Yes, Clive."

"I don't understand. If Time Flies is such a hot shot, why did Daniel sell her?"

"Because he can't afford to keep her."

"Shouldn't it be the opposite?"

"She's good enough to race in New York for some big stake money and Daniel can't afford to take her there."

"You think that young guy who bought her can?"

"He's probably an agent for someone. It's just the beginning for Time Flies. The stable fees in New York will eat up her sale price in a couple of months. It's a great day for Daniel. He bought that little mare for 500 dollars. Look at him smiling over there like he swallowed a whole bowl of cream."

I looked across the ring towards Daniel but a funny-looking gelding intercepted my line of sight. He was a sorry comical sight. His flanks were matted with manure.

All four feet were so badly overgrown that his hooves pointed upwards like skis. Strangest of all, while his body was entirely grey, his head was brown. The auctioneer appraised the horse at a glance and began.

"Do I hear a hundred dollars?" asked Fogerty flatly, his voice neglecting to include any cajoling sing-song. "Do I have a hundred dollars?"

"Guess that horse will go to the mink farm," said Grandfather without interest.

"What do you mean mink farm?"

"Minks—they eat old cows and old horses."

"That horse doesn't look so old."

"Do I hear ninety dollars?" cried Fogerty.

"Dougal will buy him for twenty-five," said Grand-father.

"Who's Dougal?"

"That fellow over there, by the gate. He always comes to the sales to pick up the scrap."

"Do I hear eighty?" called Fogerty, but there was no re-sponse.

"Couldn't someone use him for light farming?" I asked feeling sorry for the small grey horse.

"Do I hear seventy?"

"Too light. All he's good for is racing or pulling a buggy."

"Sixty?"

"A buggy? We could use him then," I said.

"Donald does fine."

"He crawls along," I said.

"So do I," said Grandpa with a smile. "We're a good match."

"Fifty."

"We could get to the store a lot faster. We could even go into Chéticamp."

"It'd still be a long drive," said Grandpa shaking his head.

"Forty dollars?" called Fogerty getting desperate. From the corner of my eye, I saw Dougal stir, himself preparing to bid. My hand shot up. Fogerty didn't miss it. "Going once at forty dollars . . . going . . . ."

"Hold it. Hold it, Fogerty," roared Grandpa. The auctioneer stopped the countdown, disappointed.

Without looking at me, Grandpa, using the bleachers as steps, walked down from our safe perch. He entered the ring and walked over to look at the horse, an old man in a worn tweed jacket and cap. I could feel the eyes of the gathered men regarding Grandfather curiously. What's he up to? Grandpa spoke to Fogerty. Fogerty nodded as if agreeing, then he held the horse by the halter while Grandpa lifted each foot and carefully examined it. Next Grandpa tipped the horse's head back and looked at the teeth. Through it all, the funny-looking horse stood patiently. Finally, Grandpa nodded and Fogerty said quietly, "Sold to William Doucet for forty dollars."

There were some broad smiles among the men as he said it—Fogerty's voice, though low, carried clearly. I ran down to meet Grandpa at the other side of the sales ring. Grandpa was just closing the gate behind him when I got there. He looked grim.

"I'm sorry," I said, but he did not reply. I tagged along after him. "Where are we going?" Grandpa paid no attention and kept walking in the direction of the stables, the brown-headed horse shuffling along behind in his little skis. He definitely seemed like a good-natured beast; a bit hollow sided, I had to admit, but obviously an easygoing disposition. We reached the wooded walk along the stables and Grandpa finally growled.

"I need another old horse like I need another hole in my head."

"How old is he?"

"Germaine is going to kill me," said Grandpa continuing to ignore me. I gave up and kept quiet.

It was as if we were at a funeral, our funeral. Grandpa stopped where the blacksmith was set up. The blacksmith, a lanky fellow, looked up from his work briefly, acknowledging our presence.

"I figure he's about thirteen," said Grandpa, speaking to no one in particular.

The blacksmith didn't respond to this interesting piece of information.

"That's young," I said surprised, thinking of Donald and Nellie who were both about twenty.

"Thirteen is over the hill for a racehorse," said the blacksmith joining in the conversation. "Now what can I do you for?" he asked, interrupting Grandfather's careful anger.

"Could you trim down the horse's feet and set a pair of shoes?"

"He's a right mess, ain't he?" said the blacksmith cheerily inspecting the brown-headed horse. "What's his name?"

"Blue Hanover," said Grandfather in a voice that was scarcely audible.

"Well Blue Hanover," said the blacksmith smiling. "I think we can fix you up. Will you, or the boy, stay by his head and steady him?"

I nodded and went quickly to hold the horse's halter while the blacksmith pulled out a monstrous pair of steel sheers. The instrument had a comic resemblance to a human nail trimmer, except these trimmers had handles about two feet long and a bite that could have removed a man's hand with one snip. The blacksmith waited until he was sure the horse was going to stand properly. He wasted no time. Snap, snap, snap—great chips of Blue Hanover's feet fell onto the wood floor. I kept waiting for him to jump from sudden pain, but the horse stood motionless. He seemed to enjoy it. Sweat stood out on the blacksmith's forehead but he worked without stopping until he dropped the last hoof with a grunt.

"Glad you're doing it," said Grandfather laconically, regarding the mounds of chips.

"Never used to see horses like this," muttered the blacksmith. "They might be a bit on the thin side but never like this. Damn lucky they pulled the shoes off him. Don't worry," smiled the blacksmith at Grandfather's worried expression. "We caught the fellow in time." And he bent down to his tool box and took out a large flat rasp which he used to smooth and shape each hoof. Once that operation was complete, he made one more tour of the horse's feet, this time with a small curved knife. Then he selected the shoes and began fitting them. I could see Grandpa visibly relax as the blacksmith drove and clinched the nails tight on the last hoof.

"How much?" asked Grandfather.

"Fifteen bucks," said the blacksmith.

"That's cheap," replied Grandfather surprised.

"I used old shoes on him," said the blacksmith stretching his stiff back. "But they should be good for four or five months. But, for God's sake, don't leave them on that long though. Pull them off in four weeks and take another crack at re-shaping the feet—they're still not quite right."

Grandfather handed the blacksmith the money and thanked him.

"Make sure he gets out on some good, damp pasture. The hoofs are brittle," the blacksmith called out as we walked away.

"I wish we had a blacksmith like you near," replied Grandfather. The blacksmith grinned and shrugged.

"Who's going to pull the shoes off him?"

"I will," said Grandfather briefly. "Peter LeVert isn't, that's for sure."

"Who's Peter LeVert?"

"Our old blacksmith—works in Boston now."

"Oh, yes. I remember you mentioning him."

The shoeing had made a dramatic difference to Blue

Hanover. He began to look like a racehorse once more. Instead of shuffling, he picked up his feet as if he didn't want to put them down for fear the "skis" would reappear. I wondered just how fast he was. Suddenly, owning Blue Hanover was becoming exciting.

Daniel and Time Flies were still the centre of attention. A group of men were clustered about them and the new owner. Dan caught a glimpse of Grandpa as we were walking by and came hurrying after us as fast as his round frame would allow.

"William. William! Is that a horse you've got there or a hat rack?"

Grandfather kept on walking, but I noticed the colour in his face heightened.

"It's Clive's horse," growled Grandfather without looking at Daniel. Daniel's broad smile swung to beam at me.

"Well you chose well. This sad sack used to be pretty speedy. Beat my horses more times than I care to admit."

"You knew the horse?" I asked surprised.

"Sure," said Daniel. "Who could forget that funny, brown head. Charlie Ferguson raced him for years in Sydney. Only horse Charlie ever owned."

"If he's so good why does he look like this?" I asked, glancing at the manure matted against Blue Hanover's quarters and his boney sides.

Daniel shrugged. "Last year, Charlie got hurt in the mine. He must have sold the horse to someone else because he always treated Blue like a baby."

Grandpa handed me a slip of paper. It said: Blue Hanover, Owner, Dr. Richard J. Morris, R.R. 4, Inverness. Not wanting to read it in front of Grandpa, I handed the note to Daniel. He looked at it briefly.

"Morris, Richard Morris." Daniel shook his head. "Don't know him. He doesn't race horses, that's for sure, otherwise I'd know him."

"Well, wherever Blue Hanover has been, he appears

sound," said Grandpa. "No sign of lame there that I can see."

"There's only one way to tell for sure," said Daniel.

"How's that?" I asked.

"Take him for a spin."

"Guess we'll do that when we get home," said Grandpa.

"In your old buggy?" exclaimed Daniel, his round face wrinkling into an applejack smile. "He'll tear it apart."

"Why?" said Grandfather mildly surprised. "He seems quiet enough."

"Not the horse, William. The speed."

"I think we'll manage," said Grandfather dryly.

"At full speed, Blue will rattle that steel-rimmed antique of yours right into match sticks," said Daniel confidently.

I looked once more at the small, boney-looking creature we had purchased and in spite of Daniel's firm conviction, I remained doubtful. So did Grandfather. Daniel must have caught our mutual expressions because he called sharply.

"Come on. Let's hitch up and we'll soon see who's right."

Grandfather hauled out his pocket watch and studied it carefully before saying regretfully, "No time. We've got to catch the taxi at five. It's four now and I must find someone to truck Blue Hanover home."

"Ah, don't worry, William. I'll take you home. I've got to truck this little filly up to Dad's anyway. There's room in the other side for your horse."

"O.K.," said Grandpa, quite pleased at the idea. "Where did you get the filly? At the auction?"

"No, from a farmer yesterday. What do you think of her, William?"

"Nice lines, but you'll have to try her out to be sure."

"Why don't we then? We've got time if we hurry."

"You're the boss," said Grandfather happily.

I stood by quietly while the two men hitched up the horses. The young filly was a roan colour; her skin flickered nervously. She looked like a kicker to me, but the harnessing was completed without incident. Grandfather eased himself into the seat while I fetched him a hard hat and goggles. Then, Daniel leading the way, they threaded a narrow path toward the track. I opened the gate and they swept into the oval. Daniel yelled something at Grandfather, he nodded, and under a tight rein, side by side, they moved around the track. Blue Hanover and Grandfather on the inside, Daniel and the young filly on the outside. A large figure joined me at the rail. It was Fogerty.

"Your Grandfather planning to start into racing?" he asked, his eyes and head focused so directly on the objects moving around the track, I wasn't sure if he was talking to me or someone further away. But there was no one else around. Most people were packing up to go home.

"No."

"Then what's he doing out there with Daniel?"

"Just trying the horse out," I said uneasily.

Fogerty shrugged as if he didn't really believe. He reached into his chest pocket and took out a package of cigarettes.

"Want one kid?"

"No thanks," I replied, a little flattered that he would consider me old enough to smoke. Fogerty lit his cigarette slowly with a contented sigh. When Daniel and Grandfather came down the homestretch for the first time, both horses were still in check. But the young filly was fighting the bit for more freedom.

"Know much about horses, son?" asked Fogerty.

"Only what Grandfather has taught me."

"That should be enough," said Fogerty his eyes still on the moving horses.

It was as if he was waiting for something to happen. I

was a diversion. Someone to keep a part of his mind focused on until he had his other business taken care of. Fogerty reminded me of a school teacher, a good school teacher, not that they would have let him within a mile of any school. He was too unorthodox, but Fogerty had an off-hand confidence that could have settled down the rowdiest classroom. He was a natural leader.

"Mr. Fogerty?"

"Yes kid."

"What will be enough?"

"Watch the horses and you'll see," he said, narrowing his eyes and his mind on to the two horses as they came around the far corner. This time as the horses came down the stretch in front of us still dead even, they were working hard. It seemed to me they were going flat out or close to it.

"Who do you think will win?" I asked Fogerty.

Instead of answering he muttered, "Next time."

"Pardon?" I said, beginning to get the hang of conversing with Fogerty.

"Next time around we'll see," said Fogerty. He reached into the front pocket of his baggy trousers and brought out a stopwatch. He studied the moving horses for a second and then clicked the watch on. For the first time, he turned his face towards me, a smile on his lips. "And unless your Grandpa can come up with some magic for that filly—it's my guess old Daniel's just bought himself a pig in a poke."

Not knowing what he meant, I nodded vaguely in agreement. Obviously delighted, Fogerty and his smile grew even wider.

Fogerty returned his attention to the track. The smile still settled on his lips.

The horses were leaning into the far turn. There was no mistaking the speed now. They were flying. The drivers were hunched forward urging the horses on.

Within a few seconds, they swept out of the final turn and into the stretch. The young filly began to move ahead. Her legs striking faster and faster. Grandpa touched Blue Hanover with the whip and, incredibly, the old campaigner responded. His whole body seemed to flatten out. His neck and head stretching, his legs pumping in a blur, and he began slowly but steadily to pull up on the outside of the younger horse. Grandpa's whip sneaked out again and the older horse edged even with Daniel, blocking him. Suddenly, the filly shot ahead, her legs stretched out in a full gallop. With a triumphant shout, Fogerty turned to me, "See! See that son! She's a breaker. Faster than greased lightning and about as useful as tits on a bull. Tell Dan that Adamson's kid used to gallop her all the time." With that bold statement, he turned on his heels, leaving me alone at the rail. I watched him disappear in the direction of the parking lot. Fogerty seemed a peculiar kind of fellow to be a mayor, but then I'd never met a mayor before. Daniel and Grandpa circled the track once more, this time at not much more than a walk, slowly cooling the horses off. I went under the rail and waited for them on the track. Daniel arrived first, flushed a jolly shade of pink. I tethered the filly against the rail.

"Well, what do you think?"

"Of what?" I asked.

"Of the colour of the sky?"

"It's blue," I said a little unsurely. Daniel shook his head sadly.

"It just looks blue." At that moment Grandfather pulled up beside us. Daniel switched his attention to Grandfather and said quietly, "Well, William. What's the diagnosis?"

Grandfather swung his legs stiffly over the edge of the sulky seat and sat there for a moment. His back to Blue Hanover. His feet dangling comfortably.

"The diagnosis, *mon cher ami,* is that you're right."

"I am, damn!" said Daniel with feeling.

"I need a new buggy," said Grandpa with a twinkle.

Daniel burst out laughing.

"You may laugh," said Grandpa gravely, "but these days, finding a buggy that still has rubber tires is no joke. They're as scarce as hen's teeth."

"Tell you what William, I'll find you one somewhere if you'll cure the filly of breaking."

Grandpa considered this for a moment and said, "O.K., it's a deal." They shook hands.

"Mr. Deveau?"

"Don't call me Mr. Deveau; Daniel's my name."

"Yes sir," I said cautiously. "Mr. Fogerty had a message for you."

"Yes?" asked Daniel, his attention surging full on me.

"He said to tell you that Adamson's kid used to gallop her all the time."

"Damn! Why didn't he tell me before I bought her?"

"Ah, you guessed she was a breaker," said Grandpa. "You can't have everything. Fogerty just played his side of the game. You'll have the last laugh yet."

"You think so?" said Daniel doubtfully.

"Sure," said Grandpa confidently. "With a little luck, come next spring you've got another three-thousand-dollar filly."

"That's what I hoped when I bought her," said Daniel. "But, I'm not so sure now. I was waiting for her to break coming down the stretch and I still couldn't stop her. As soon as Blue started to pressure her, she cracked."

"*Mon dieu.* Give the filly a chance, Daniel."

"Patience has never been a virtue of mine," replied Daniel dryly. We slowly walked over to his truck and un-hitched the horses by the tailgate. Then, as Daniel packed away the equipment, Grandfather and I rubbed the two horses down. It was a task I always enjoyed. The horses, resting comfortably, enjoyed the attention. For a moment as I watched Grandfather curry Blue Hanover, it struck me that with some decent feed, a little attention and a few weeks' time, he would be a very fine-looking horse—although he'd always be a bit comical with that brown head of his. I went back to my work thinking again about Fogerty, and wondering why he had seemed so pleased. Galloping a trotting horse would ruin it for sulky racing—even I knew that.

"Clive?"

"Yes Grandpa."

"Thanks for putting your hand up at the sale."

"You're not mad at me any more?"

"I'm very happy. All my life I've wanted to own a driving horse, something really fancy, but there never seemed to be enough money."

Grandpa's voice trailed off and he absentmindedly pushed at a rough spot on Blue Hanover's side.

"When you've got a large family and a small farm, luxuries like Blue here are hard to justify."

"What about when the children were gone?" I asked.

"By that time, it seemed like a foolish indulgence. I was sixty-six or seven before Armand left."

"How old was Grandma when she had her last baby?" I asked.

"Fifty," said Grandpa. Then he returned to currying Blue Hanover. I went back to my work and so we continued in silence until the job was finished.

"Ready to go?" called Daniel from the back of the truck.

"They should be cooled down a bit more," replied Grandpa.

"Hell, William, what do you think this is—New York? Throw a blanket across them. Let's roll."

Grandpa shrugged and we loaded them, a flashy green and gold blanket across each horse's back. Daniel wheeled the truck and the double horse trailer out of the park like he was driving a sports car. Inside the cab, rock music wrapped us up while the countryside rolled by, the sweet smell of hay and horse flesh clinging to the whole show. Grandpa's and Daniel's voices buzzed quietly in the background.

I was asleep when we got home.

Politics

Politics is a dangerous subject. I learned that the hard way or, more to the point, Grandfather did. It seems curious, looking back, that my first contact with the dangerous world of politics would have occurred in the village, not in Ottawa. But my dad took care to keep political matters where they belonged—in someone else's house. Dad was and still is an economist. He took his profession and his vocation, the Public Service, seriously and one of the peripheral obligations of being a civil servant in Ottawa was to steer clear of politics. Consequently, parliament and politicians were never discussed. Dad was very strict about it. His job was to advise the government, not to take sides. That was his bottom, middle and top line in the political game, although around election time there would certainly be some rumblings from Mother's corner about Ottawa being a city of political eunuchs and so on. Nevertheless, Dad's wishes were respected. Politics, politicians and political parties were left to other people. There could have been pink elephants running the country for all I knew. To this day I'm not sure how Dad votes. But Grandfather didn't have such delicate reservations. He was a Liberal. He had always voted Liberal and always would vote Liberal.

Nineteen fifty-eight was a difficult time for Liberals and Grandfather was no exception. Diefenbaker had taken the country by storm. The Tories were in power. His own sons were openly voting Conservative and the

whole country was going to hell. Grandfather didn't trust
Diefenbaker. The man was a nincompoop and besides it
galled him to see Gilles LeVert getting the trucking con-
tracts while Gerard was sitting idle.

In Grand Etang it didn't matter what your race, religion or language was (although there was about a ninety-
nine percent chance it would be white, Catholic and
French) but your politics—that was something else. That
was a matter of choice. And Grandpa considered anyone
a damn fool who chose to be a Tory. Fortunately for
Grandpa, most of the time it wasn't much of a problem
because the Tories usually sat where they deserved—in
"the bleachers," as Grandpa fondly called the opposition
side of the House. Tories, Liberals—they were people,
people you voted for and sent to Ottawa to represent
you. If your side won, you got a bridge or harbour works
built. If your side lost, you didn't. The worst damn thing
that could happen to you was to have a Tory government
and a Liberal elected in your riding or vice-versa.

That was the cynical view of politics. Grandpa pre-
ferred the high-minded view. Winning was not important. Voting for the best party was all that counted. The
Liberals were always the best. Sadly, unbelievably, in
1958, his beloved Liberals were sitting in the bleachers.
Consequently at the very mention of politics, Grandpa
would sink into despair. Glum. No, not just glum—the
very picture of glumness, his cloth cap barely visible
above the up-turned collar of his coat. The classrooms of
the "Nation's Capital" may not have taught me much
about politics, but I could recognize a mark at five
hundred yards in a blizzard. And on politics Grandpa
was an irresistible mark. Our last trip around the political bush happened like this:

It was Grandfather's habit to stable the colt in the stall
next to Nellie. Grandfather was feeding her a mixture of
oats and bran as a supplement to help her regain

strength. I was sitting on the edge of the manger with the colt, talking in a rather loud voice so that Grandfather could hear me on the other side of the wooden partition. I was going on about how this here fellow, Pearson, couldn't be all that bad seeing he had won the Nobel Peace Prize and all. This pleased Grandfather, as I knew it would, because Lester Pearson was a Liberal. Grandfather rose faithfully, took the bait, hook, line and sinker. He held forth at great length on the many virtues of Lester B. and most particularly the fine qualities of the Liberal Party and Mr. Mackenzie King, to whom Mr. Pearson obviously owed a great deal.

After some reflection I was inclined to disagree with this, noting that Mr. Pearson had won his Nobel Prize prior to entering politics. In fact, he had been a public servant at the time. If anything, I stated judiciously, and with growing confidence, Mr. Pearson had gone downhill. Noting that since entering politics he was inclined to waffle and waver. At least one knew where one stood with Mr. Diefenbaker. Diefenbaker said what he meant, and meant what he said, or so I had been told by Uncle Phil. There was a brief silence while Grandpa digested these treasonous statements. In a few moments I had praised the Tories as well as the wretched and pompous Mr. Diefenbaker, spoken ill of Mr. Pearson's fine qualities and his association with the Liberals and implied that an adult member of the family was the source of these nefarious opinions. The explosion came. Grandfather refused to listen further.

"If you can't speak sense, Clive, don't speak at all. And . . ." The curry comb he was using to groom old Nellie fairly flew back and forth across her back. Small clouds of dust puffed up from the vigour of his stroke. And I was in stitches from trying not to laugh out loud. Now, while both Grandfather and I were preoccupied out-loud with our own particular vices, neither of us noticed that both

Nellie and the colt were getting increasingly nervous at all this shouting and carrying on. The old mare nickered softly for her colt and the little one shuffled back and forth. Heedless, I had fallen completely into the manger and was giggling insanely. I barely had the strength to administer the coup de grâce.

"When I grow up, Grandpa, I think I'll vote Tory."

"Tory! I won't have a damn Tory in my house," cried Grandpa, beside himself with rage. He turned and began to stamp out of the stall to confront me directly with the move-out-or-vote-Liberal ultimatum, but Grandpa didn't quite make it. Nellie kicked him flat up against the harness which was hanging on the opposite wall. He fell heavily to the floor. My laughter turned to fear. I scrambled to help him up. Grandpa gingerly tried to put some weight on his leg. It held. By some miracle, his leg did not seem to be broken. He rolled up his pant leg to reveal an ugly red swelling that had already begun around the knee cap.

"Damn horse has got more sense than we have," grunted Grandfather. "Still can't have her going around kicking people. Hand me that board."

"The two-by-four?"

"The two-by-four," said Grandpa grimly, and I passed it to him. He supported himself by standing on his good leg and leaning against the edge of the stall. The two-by-four hit Nellie's rear end with a resounding whack. Her hind legs flew straight up under the impact, but she didn't kick. Grandpa stopped to catch his breath and rub his knee. Then he whacked her again. I couldn't quite figure out which hurt more, his knee or his pride.

"Poor old soul," said Grandfather when he was finished. Both he and the old mare were trembling like leaves. "Now, do you see where talking about politics gets you, Clive? Nowhere. Now go into the house and get me a peppermint."

I ran to the house, uncertain whether to laugh or cry.

When I returned Nellie was grazing peacefully in the night pasture with the colt by her side. Grandfather was sitting on the barrel by the mare's stall, pensive and quiet. He accepted the peppermint gracefully. I wondered out loud if we should go to a doctor. He shook his head and then said, "Not a word about this to Germaine. Not a word, Clive. She has enough to worry about." I nodded dumbly but asked how we could explain the limp.

"I hit it with a hammer," said Grandfather, hesitating. ". . . repairing a wheel."

"Yes," I said rather dubiously, while thinking Aunt Germaine would not believe the story. On the other hand, would she believe the real thing? I sucked on my peppermint.

It's been a long time since I was that little boy who teased his grandpa. I've had more education than you could shake a stick at. I've taken courses in Political Sociology and Political Science from professors who specialize in that line of thought. I've learned to use a different vocabulary from Grandfather—the institutionalization of the adversary system, and what-not—but I haven't learned much that is new.

In the city, Sunday is a kind of left-over-day. Not quite a Monday, not quite a Saturday and a long way from Friday—a left-over day. It wasn't the same in Grand Etang. Sunday in the village had character and substance. It was an important day. Except for the absolute essentials like milking, all work was suspended. There was church in the morning and I learned that Sunday didn't have to be sombre. There were friends to meet, plans to be laid, jokes to be told. In the village, the Catholic faith had sense of humour, and as the summer wore on I had grown to quite like Sunday. It was a day to look forward to.

One more week to go and then it was back to the city,

back to school. I laid my axe down and looked at the two horses, both saddled and bridled, waiting patiently. Father Marinelli was expected. We were supposed to go for a leisurely Sunday afternoon ride, a prospect I normally would have looked upon with pleasure. The priest was a fine rider and good company. I chopped away at the wood absentmindedly, the blows coming with a practiced sweep. It passed the time. I wasn't really working. My axe stuck in the wood. I levered it free and swung once more, this time hard and fast. The axe ricocheted off a hard knot in the wood, twisted out of my hand and buried itself in the top of my leather boot. Clearly it seemed to have happened. I had hurt myself, yet there was no pain. For a moment I wondered if I really had cut myself. Then the dark arterial blood began to pump up between the boot laces, soaking my sock and boot. I sat down and the flow eased a bit, but not much. With each beat of my heart the blood bubbled up. I clamped my hand down on the cut, too afraid to take my boot off. Just then Grandfather came out of the house. "Grandpa! Grandpa!" He strolled up the little hill towards me, full of Sunday dinner.

"Grandpa! I cut my foot."

"Let's see," said Grandpa calmly. I took my hand away and the blood pulsed up once more in a thick crimson clot. He turned without saying anything and ran back down the hill to the house. Germaine came out. I heard him say, "I'll get the car," whereupon he began to run in an elfish seventy-eight-year-old run towards our closest neighbours, the Leblancs, forgetting in his excitement there were horses tethered and ready to go by the barn. I called to him but the on-shore wind carried my voice back to me. Grandpa did not hear me. It was all quite comical I told myself except the blood wouldn't stop slowing no matter how hard I pressed.

"Dear me," said Aunt Germaine and she unbuttoned

her apron and folded it up. "Try pressing this against it."

"Shall I take my boot off?" I asked.

"No. Better leave that for the doctor," she said.

"O.K.," I said obligingly. "Are we going to Chéticamp?"

"Yes. Please keep your foot up, Clive."

"Yes, aunt." We sat together in silence and watched the blood leak out between my fingers. "Shouldn't we put a tourniquet on it or something?" I said vaguely.

"No. Just keep your hand pressed against it."

"Yes, Aunt." We waited, neither of us wanting to look at my boot and neither able to do anything else. For once, the sky offered no comfort, remote and uncomprehending. I had an image of a mouse dying. A car came bouncing down the lane towards the house. Everything was going to be all right. Arthur's eldest son, Peter, was driving. Peter helped me into the back seat of the car. Once safely inside the car, away from the expanding pool of blood around my boot, the tight, panicky feeling in my chest began to fade. Everything was going to be fine. Chéticamp Hospital was only six or seven miles away. Surely I wouldn't die so close to a hospital?

"Clive, try not to get any blood on the seat," said Aunt Germaine. "Here are some towels. Put them under your boot."

"Yes, Aunt."

"It's O.K.," said Peter and the car lurched onto the highway. I was definitely not panicky any more but I began to wonder about this fading business. Everything kept fading. My tongue, my eyes. Where did I live? No, that was for a concussion. I had better say a prayer. What prayer? The only one I could remember was, "Hail Mary, full of grace." I had never liked "Hail Mary, full of grace." It had always struck me as kind of a silly prayer. The car lurched around a curve.

"Peter, it's not going to help if you kill us on the way," said Aunt Germaine shrilly.

"Hail Mary, full of grace," I prayed to myself. "And I take back the silly part." That was the last thing I remembered in the car.

When I woke up I was on the operating table. The doctor was peering at my foot, and when he noticed I had revived, he said, "Oh, hello. You did a nice job, didn't you?"

Standing Guard

"A dance? I don't want to go to a dance," I stated uncategorically. "Besides, I don't think I can. The stitches only came out yesterday."

"You don't have to go," said Aunt Germaine calmly.

"Stay home and watch T.V. if you wish." And she left me to contemplate the joys of watching television alone. Grandfather came out of his bedroom carrying his shaving gear. I watched him set up by the sink. It never ceased to fascinate me. I couldn't for the life of me figure out how he avoided slitting his throat with the naked blade. It made me nervous just to watch.

"You going to the dance too Grandpa?"

"Wouldn't miss it."

"I'm not going."

"Why is that?" said Grandfather as he whipped the soap into a frothing, white lather around his face.

It wasn't a hard question to answer. I had only been to one dance before. We had all stood around in the gym while some records played. A couple of kids danced and then we all went home.

"Doesn't seem much point to it," I said.

"I see," replied Grandfather, paying careful attention to his shaving.

"What's this dance for?" I asked, anxious in spite of my objections.

"No reason," said Grandfather.

"See what I mean," I replied.

202 My Grandfather's Cape Breton

Unperturbed, Grandfather continued his careful shaving. I got up to leave. "Hold it," called Grandfather. "Hold it. I believe there is a reason. Marie mentioned something to me on the phone."

"What is it?"

"Pierre, Marie-Hélène's husband, had a good week fishing. Caught almost seven hundred dollars worth of lobster.

"I see," I said. "So this is sort of a celebration, like when we finished Grade Eight."

"That's it."

"Will there be any kids at the dance?"

"Just a minute." said Grandfather. I waited while Grandfather managed to nick his upper lip. "Damn! I should have known better."

"What's the matter?"

"I shave better when I'm not talking. Pass me that little stick."

"This?"

"Yes."

"What is it?"

"Stops the bleeding." Grandfather applied some and winced as he did so. "It stings," he said succinctly.

"Why don't you use a safety razor like Dad. They seem a lot less dangerous."

"A straight razor's better," said Grandfather bluntly. "With these little box razors you're shaving every five minutes. Not good for the skin." Then Grandpa toweled his face off. "Besides I'm to old to change."

"You certainly look scrubbed," I conceded.

"That I do. Now to put on my dancing shoes."

"What are your dancing shoes?"

"Same ones I wear to church," said Grandpa with a grin and headed back to his bedroom.

"You didn't tell me if there were going to be any kids at the dance."

"There'll be kids, André, Roland, Joe Chiasson."

"Roland and Joe are going? What are they going for?"

"To cause trouble, I imagine," said Grandpa faking a grim look.

"I think I'll go."

"You find causing trouble attractive?"

"Sure," I replied cheerfully. "Be ready in two secs."

It didn't take us long to get to Pierre and Marie Le-Vert's place. They lived in a small house about two miles from our house. Old Donald could make it in 15 minutes without trying very hard at all. Although I had passed their house many times on the way to the bakery, I had never been in. It was a very modest, unpainted house and barn situated in a small pocket of land. The house itself was surrounded by an orchard. The trees gave the grounds a wonderful, secretive green texture, quite different from the naked horizons that surrounded our farm. From the lights and noise from the house, the dance was already well underway. I helped Aunt Germaine down. The grass underfoot felt lush and Donald was already picking at it. "I'll unhitch," I called to Grandpa.

"O.K. Put him on a long lead and throw the white blanket over him. I don't want someone with too much to drink cracking him with a car."

"Why don't I put him at the bottom of the orchard then. They can't drive that far."

"Perfect," replied Grandpa. I walked Donald, protesting, down to the edge of the orchard. I guess he thought there was less grass at this further end, but if anything it seemed richer than the higher ground. I tethered him quickly and made my way back towards the light and music. The lane and yard were jammed with cars. Soft, buttery light from kerosene lamps lighted the path to the back door. I rounded the corner of the house and ran smack into Roland.

"What took you so long?"

"Have you seen Joe or André?" I countered.

"No, I haven't seen Joe or André," grumbled Roland.

"What's the matter with you?" I asked, curious. Roland was usually so good natured.

"Nothing."

"Well let's go inside then. . . . Where exactly is the dance anyway?"

"It's in the kitchen, like at your Aunt Germaine's birthday party."

"People around here sure seem to do a lot of dancing." I replied tentatively.

"At the drop of a hat," replied Roland in full complaint. "And come fall, it gets worse."

"Is there any food?"

"It's not out yet."

"Have they got any horses here?" I asked, getting a bit desperate.

"Monsieur LeVert used to keep a couple of horses. I don't know if he still does. Let's go check in the barn."

"O.K.," I said, happy also to be delayed from entering the frantic adult activity of dancing. We went around to the side of the barn where the horse stable was located. The door was ajar. It struck me as curious and with an automatic reflex I shut it after us. The horse stalls, chains, harness were still there—but no horses. Everything was in good repair. It looked like the animals had just left. I checked the manger to be sure, but it was empty and dry. It had been awhile since Mr. LeVert had kept horses.

"Look at this," called Roland further inside the barn. "A two seater, I've never seen one before."

"A two-seater what?" I demanded peering into the dusky light.

"A two-seater buggy, you dope. What do you think Monsieur LeVert used to drive—a sports car?" My eyes began to adjust to the tiny light and I began to see the outline of the buggy. It certainly was impressive. A double hitch, upholstered seats, two people sitting in the back seat. Two people sitting in the seat? I almost jumped out of my skin. In the same instant, Roland saw them and crashed into me in his hurry to get pointed towards the exit. We fell down in a jumble of arms and legs, completely panicked.

"Welcome to the party boys!" A familiar voice boomed out. It was David Boudreau.

"Come and sit up here. There's plenty of room in the front seat. Come on, don't be afraid. It's just me, and Sylvia."

"What are you doing in here?" asked Roland.

"Just talking," said David—and holding hands, my eyes recorded dutifully.

"Stop acting like little policemen," said David sounding a bit annoyed. "Come up here and I'll tell you a story."

"O.K.," I said, always eager to hear one of David's stories. Roland climbed more reluctantly into the seat behind me.

"Are you ready lads?" We nodded. "Ready Sylvia?"

"Ready," said Sylvia.

"Well, this story is about buried treasure," said David quietly. "And it's a true one." I listened as David's voice blended perfectly with the moonlight coming in through the small window above the carriage.

"You boys are too young to remember this but the Boudreau family wasn't always as poor and wayward as it is today. You know that big house down by the school? Six bedrooms on the second floor and two on the third. Well, that's where I was born. Dad was one of the wealthiest men in the village. It's true—you ask your Grand-dad if you don't believe me. Old Michael David Boudreau owned a seventy-foot boat, a couple of hundred acres of the best farmland. In those days, I didn't shamble around to work on other people's property. People came to the Boudreaus'. And Dad usually had a spot for a good man. Even in the Thirties he always had something on the go. When I was ten, I remember we had eighteen people on the farm in two separate houses. Isn't that something?"

"What happened?" I asked, thinking of the tiny cabin David Boudreau now lived in.

"Well, it started when my grandmother died. I must have been nine or ten at the time. Dad was appointed the executor of her estate, which didn't amount to a great deal. She lived with us at the time and had nothing more than a few trunks and what-not. Anyway, Dad went through her things as he was supposed to, to see who should get what and in his search he came across these letters all bundled up in ribbon. Well, Dad had half a mind to just chuck them all in the stove for he didn't want to be reminded of the past. But he hesitated to because by rights they didn't belong to him. They belonged to the family. So he went through each and every letter. It gradually became clear that they weren't just letters from the recent past, between Grandma and Grandpa, but a continuous family history that went back to the time of the dispersion over two hundred years ago. Well you can imagine how excited Dad was. Funny thing was, he didn't really want to part with them, but after some time my mother persuaded him to show them around the family, which he did. And eventually a museum fella from Halifax got wind of them and came up to see Dad, and that's where those letters of Grandma's are now—in Halifax in the museum. And if you don't believe that, next time you go to Halifax with the school, drop into the museum and ask for the Boudreaus' letters. That's where they are, under a glass case marked 'Boudreau letters,' or at least that's where most of them are. Dad kept two of them and those two letters eventually were the cause of the whole Boudreau family downfall."

"What was in them?"

"Well, it was a long time before anyone realized some old pieces of paper were the root of all our family troubles. And when we did it was too late!"

"What happened?" asked Roland, rising equally to the bait.

"Well Dad started to take these mysterious trips. He'd be away from the house for weeks at a time. He would just leave never explaining how long he'd be gone or why. He'd just go. Mother began to go a bit crazy trying to handle the family, the farm and everything else. She just couldn't do it. The fishing business was the first to go. A distant cousin took pity on my mother and offered to buy the boat. My mother says he stole it for a song. Then the butcher shop went—the Chiassons *à* Marc André bought it—they still run it today."

"Couldn't your mother find out where your father was going?"

"Yes, she did eventually, but by then it was too late."

"Well?" asked Sylvia, leaning forward with an impish grin. "Tell us what happened."

"Mother hired two men, Michel and Ulric Arsenault. They were the hunters in the village, and they tracked father clear across to the east coast of the island, where they found he had a camp set up in this cove and a regular quarry started around it. Father had settled down to work in this isolated spot just like he was in his own backyard. Every now and then he would stop his picking and shovelling to consult a piece of paper he carried in his wallet. Well, Michel and Ulric weren't any wiser as to what was going on and there was no one around to ask, so they decided to try and steal the piece of paper. They figured it was a map of some sort and would bring it home to my mother. They waited in the woods until it was past midnight, then stole down to the little cabin Father had built. His trousers were hanging on the back of the door with the wallet still attached to Dad's belt. Michel didn't want to try and take the papers out of the pouch for fear of waking father so he took the belt off and left the trousers. Once he was outside he left the trousers on a bench. Then he and Ulric hightailed it home. They didn't even bother to look at the papers until they arrived safely in our kitchen."

"What was in them?"

"It wasn't a map as they had thought. They were just two letters. They were written by a Martin Boudreau at the time of the fall of Louisbourg. Well, this Martin Boudreau had managed to escape through the English blockade as a crew member on a small sailing vessel of a rich, French official. They sailed towards the North with the intention of making straight across the Atlantic for France but the ship was caught in a terrible storm that shipwrecked them, on the coast somewhere between Ingonish and St. Ann's. The storm hammered the little ship on a reef for two days and two nights and at the end of it Martin Boudreau was the only survivor. Somehow he was carried by the waves clean over the rocks and into a small cave. The two letters father had were the story of his escape and his subsequent wanderings before he settled in the village not far from the house I was born in."

"What about the treasure?" asked Roland getting down to brass tacks.

"Well, as you can imagine, after the storm the small cove was littered with debris. Dead men, spars, sailcloth, pieces of foredeck—he describes it all quite clearly in his letters—and one iron-bound chest filled with gold coins. Martin Boudreau couldn't lift the chest so he stripped the clothes off the dead men and buried bags of gold back under the trees. And that's what my Dad had been looking for all this time—gold wrapped in dead men's clothing."

"Did he find the gold?"

"No, he never did. He made a couple of trips back to the cove which he thought was the one Martin Boudreau had described in his letters, but he never did find any hint of gold."

"So he gave up?"

"Yes; it seemed once people knew what he was doing, he lost interest in the search himself. Besides, I think he was ashamed. Once he had shifted his eyes from the treasure hunting, he began to realize how badly the family's fortunes were reduced in the village."

"He still had the big farm," I said practically.

"He lost that too eventually."

"How?" I asked curiously. "You can't lose a farm—it doesn't go anywhere." David Boudreau laughed at my naive reply.

"I suppose you're right, lad. It sounds strange, but there are easy enough ways to lose a farm and Dad found 'em. It wasn't very hard. By the time I was sixteen, Dad was a day-labourer just like I am now and the whole family had scattered like so many seeds in the wind."

"What happened?" asked Roland bewildered.

"I guess Dad was always more of a businessman than a farmer. He wasn't that interested in farming. The farm was just a home for him, so he took a mortgage out against the farm to get himself started in another business. A hotel it was, up by the point. Built it himself, but it only lasted two years, and when it failed, the bank collected on the farm. Simple enough, eh lads?"

"Did anyone else go looking for the gold?"

"Not that I know of."

"Why not?"

"Some people say it's because shipwreck gold is cursed."

"That's foolish," I said resolutely.

"Probably is," answered David equably. "More likely it's because shipwreck gold is a good deal harder to find than the stories."

"Have you ever seen that cove your father was digging in?"

"Several times."

"Would you take us there?" asked Roland brazenly

"Sure, but you'd have to do me a favour first."

"What's that?" we asked simultaneously.

"Stand guard by the barn door, so that Sylvia and I can have a few moments to ourselves."

"Will do," said Roland, cheerily disembarking from the front seat.

And so we spent the rest of the evening resolutely guarding the stable door; resisting all entreaties by Joe and André to do otherwise.

"What's the matter, Clive?"

"Nothing."

"You've been sitting here for a long time."

"Just watching the sun go down," I said.

Grandfather chose a block of wood not far from me and he, too, sat down. He said nothing. And together we watched the last remnants of the sun's light retreat across the sea until the red protest disappeared.

"Your grandmother loved to watch the sun set. She used to sit in a lawn chair over there—I guess I've told you that—I should take time to watch it more often."

"You're spoiled, Grandpa," I said jokingly. "In Ottawa you could live your whole life and never see a sunset like that."

"So your father tells me. But sunsets don't pay the rent."

"Yes, he says that too," I replied with a grudging smile.

"Clive?"

"Yes, Grandpa."

"I'm an old man now."

"You're not that old," I protested, upset at the thought.

"Well, the fact is I am seventy-eight. Not ancient, mind you, but I'm well down the trail. And so is my poor old farm. Did you know it used to be twice this size. I sold a good chunk of it last year. All that high country towards Levi's is sold. We had the mill. This place isn't much more than a hobby for me now. A hobby I love, mind you. But still a hobby. Nothing much will get disturbed if my old horses go. No—don't interrupt. It's our last evening and I want to tell you some things.

"I've got it pretty easy now. I putter around with my grandchildren when they visit and we have a fine time together. I've got more horses than I need and less cows than I should. If I want I can watch the sun going down instead of racing away from it on some business that just can't wait. But when I was your Dad's age, things were different. Your grandmother and ten children depended on me and this little farm. I worked as if there would be no tomorrow. It gave us a good life, but demanded a great deal. In turn, I demanded much from my children, especially the boys. Often I didn't give them much except a short temper." Grandfather looked down at his large, work-hardened hands. "I guess what I'm trying to say is don't judge your father by this old fellow. He's much better than I am."

"I'll be glad to see Mom and Dad," I said quietly. "But I'm still not sure I want to go back."

"Why not?"

"It's hard to explain."

"Try."

"It's not just Dad expecting too much. It's everyone. I'm supposed to do well in school because of a test I took,

but I'm not doing very well. I have to repeat Grade Eight.
Mom and Dad expect me to be responsible because I'm
the oldest. Teachers expect me to do well in sports because I'm big. I seem to spend all my time doing well or
trying to do well so I won't feel afraid. There never seems
to be any time to be me. Whoever that is?"

"Maybe you're expecting too much yourself," said
Grandfather quietly. "Ah, but how should I know eh?
Things were different when I was your age. In my day,
there wasn't much choice. You were either a farmer or a
fisherman and that was that."

"And now you can't be either," I said, my voice carrying farther than I had intended in the quiet twilight.

"That's a fact," said Grandfather blithely. "Only a fool
would want a little place like this. Any idea what you want
to be when you grow up?"

"A lawyer," I said without hesitating.

"A lawyer," said Grandfather, moving cautiously
around the word as if it was a bit hot. In Grand Etang
lawyers generally meant trouble. Marriage trouble, last
will and testament trouble, boundary trouble. Trouble.

"I was just kidding, Grandpa. I don't know what I want
to be. But if I say I want to be a lawyer it keeps grown-ups
quiet. I was just practising. I don't want to be a lawyer."

"I've never asked you before," said Grandfather, a bit
hurt.

"I didn't mean you, Grandpa. You know that." We sat
for a while longer in companionable silence. "Grandpa?"

"Yes."

"Do you know what I would like to be when I grow
up?"

"I thought that was a forbidden subject," said Grandfather warily.

"I just thought of it."

"O.K. What?"

"A conductor of dinosaurs."

"*Alors, trouves ton dinosaure,*" said Grandfather reasonably.

"Of course—find my dinosaur," I replied with a big smile. Grandfather smiled. Then for no particular reason, we began to laugh and laugh and laugh until the tears rolled down our cheeks.

"I'm going to miss you, Grandpa," I finally gasped. "Miss you a whole lot."

"And I you," said Grandfather.

"Could I come back next summer?"

"Of course. If you want I'll drive old Donald all the way to Ottawa to pick you up."

"I'll be waiting a long time if you do. Better take Blue Hanover. You'll get there faster."

"Right," said Grandpa, his cheeks creased with tears. He stood up a bit stiffly. "Brrr. It's getting cool. Let's go inside."

"Yes it is." I stood up and we began to walk down the small hill towards the house.